**How to Avoid Business Failure**

HELEN BEARE was born in 1963 in Plymouth. After a degree in French and German at Cambridge University, she worked for a firm of chartered accountants in London, later specializing in working with smaller businesses and in business planning. She now lives near Buckingham, working with her partner in a chartered accountancy practice established by him in 1989.

*Sheldon Business Books*

Sheldon Business Books is a list which exists to promote and facilitate the adoption of humane values and equal opportunities integrated with the technical and commercial expertise essential for successful business practice. Both practical and theoretical issues which challenge today's workforce will be explored in jargon-free, soundly researched books.

The first titles in the series are:
*Making Change Work for You* by Alison Hardingham
*Taking the Macho Out of Management* by Paddy O'Brien
*How to Succeed in Psychometric Tests* by David Cohen
*Fit to Work* by Paddy O'Brien

Helen Beare **How to Avoid Business Failure**

Sheldon Business Books

First published in Great Britain 1993
Sheldon Press, SPCK, Marylebone Road, London NW1 4DU

© Helen Beare 1993

British Library Cataloguing-in-Publication Data
A catalogue record for this book is available from the British Library
ISBN 0-85969-676-6

Typography by Daniel Edwards
Photoset by Deltatype Ltd, Ellesmere Port, Cheshire
Printed in Great Britain at the University Press, Cambridge

# Contents

**For the three P's**

## Acknowledgements

I would like to thank all those involved in small businesses who have so willingly discussed their successes and failures with me and offered thoughts based on their own experiences. Thanks are also due to Paul for his feedback and practical comments.

Thanks to the following for permission to reproduce or adapt copyright material: McGraw-Hill Book Company (UK) Limited; John Wiley & Sons; The Institute of Chartered Accountants in England & Wales; W H Allen & Co plc; Weidenfeld & Nicolson. Thanks also to G A Purkis at the Department of Trade and Industry for supplying me with statistical information on business failure rates.

I'd also like to thank my editor, Joanna Moriarty, for her support and enthusiasm over the past year. Lastly, especial thanks to my partner, Neil Priddy, for providing unfailing moral and intellectual support throughout.

# Introduction

A vast amount has been written on the subject of business management providing advice on the smooth running of a business under normal trading conditions. There exists little guidance for coping when things are not going well.

Nobody wants to admit that their business is facing severe difficulties, whatever the cause. Owners and managers of smaller businesses in particular may lack the experience or expertise to recognize problems at an early enough stage, and, more importantly, to know how to deal with them.

The reality is that businesses are failing in increasing and alarming numbers, often with devastating effects for the personal finances of their owners, managers and employees, as well as the knock-on effects for customers and suppliers. There can be few small businesses in existence which have not had contact with one which has failed.

In a gloomy economic climate, it is often felt that the fate of many small businesses rests on the economy as a whole. To a degree this is true, but the business owner or manager can still make a significant contribution to the future of the business and of those associated with it. The decisions and actions of the individual who controls its overall operations can make the difference between failure and survival, or in the worst case, between a straightforward winding-up and personal ruin.

There is no such thing as a miracle cure for a business which is suffering declining performance, and this book does not set out to look for one. What is important is to learn how to recognize the danger signs at an early stage, and to understand how to decide on the most constructive course of action.

To help owners and managers of smaller businesses to achieve this aim, the book looks not only at the financial symptoms of failure, but also at aspects of management style and common operating problems experienced in failing businesses. As well as drawing on some of the theory developed by business failure experts, this is applied to examples both of failed businesses and those which have survived their problems. Issues such as financial planning and accounting control are also covered, as these are often neglected and handled on a 'fire-fighting' basis when a business is struggling for survival.

There are, of course, circumstances where additional professional advice will be required in attempting to identify and resolve a business's difficulties. Again, it is important to recognize when extra support is needed, and to know where to look for it.

The overall aim of this book is to emphasize the necessity of recognizing business problems as early as possible and, by analysing the causes, to suggest courses of action. It takes a practical approach and above all stresses that a head-in-the-sand attitude towards difficulties is probably the quickest route to failure.

# 1. Business failure

Businesses fail not only in periods of poor trading conditions but in all economic climates, although the issue naturally receives most attention when the number of companies entering liquidation is sufficiently high to provoke real concern. The reasons for failure are less widely discussed unless a suspicion of fraud exists or the failing company is large enough and the consequences sufficiently far-reaching for the failure to become a matter of general public interest. Individual and smaller company failures are often mentioned only as statistics, although their combined effect on the economy is significant.

The level of liquidations, receiverships and bankruptcies in England and Wales in the early 1990s has risen dramatically, as the effects of a prolonged period of adverse economic conditions spread to all sectors of the economy. Company liquidations in the year to March 1992 rose to 22,719, compared with 17,164 in the previous twelve-month period, and personal bankruptcies increased to 29,289 from 16,481. These figures are likely to rise further, as businesses which had anticipated an improvement in economic conditions find that they cannot survive an additional period of unfavourable economic pressures. Even when these pressures have subsided and conditions improved, a large number of businesses, and particularly small ones, remain extremely vulnerable. Economic recovery as measured by government statistics does not lead to the swift recovery of a business which has struggled to remain afloat for several years.

The use of the term 'business failure' can be confusing: it has become increasingly adopted as a blanket term to cover receiverships, liquidations (either voluntary or compulsory) and bankruptcies, as well as a descriptive term for businesses which perform poorly. In a period of recession, the number of businesses which are failing in terms of their poor performance can be far higher than the number which have entered liquidation and become legally dissolved. Obviously, published business failure statistics provide a concrete indication of past failure trends, but they are unable to reflect the additional numbers of businesses on the brink of failure.

It is worthwhile examining the various ways in which the term 'business failure' is used, and the implications of different types of failure.

In a descriptive sense, business failure for a publicly quoted company can refer to a project or a company which fails to realize a return on investment or capital judged to be satisfactory by its investors. Investors may make this judgement by reference to the returns achieved by similar projects or companies, or to projections of future performance. Rates of return will vary according to prevailing economic and market conditions, but if the rate is continually lower than comparable investments, the project or company may be judged a failure. In spite of this failure, the company may continue for a long period to trade and to pay its creditors without undue problems.

For a company not quoted on the Stock Exchange, a number of measures may initially be used as indicators of the success or failure of a business. Where, for example, gross profit margins consistently fall short of those projected in the company's planning process or show a decline compared with earlier years, this often indicates a lack of control in the day-to-day management of the company's operations. In periods of economic downturn, it can also result from pressures to reduce selling prices in order to stimulate sales. The same is often true where actual liquid resources, mainly cash, continually fall short of what is needed to meet current financial liabilities, such as payments to trade creditors. In such cases, bank overdrafts and other sources of credit are increasingly extended to meet obligations to creditors. Again, a company experiencing these problems may continue to trade, even if unsatisfactorily. Although it may not enter liquidation, its poor results and weak financial position can classify it as a failure in terms of its financial performance.

A number of other measures may be adopted as indicators of the potential failure of a business, and these are examined in more detail in chapter 6.

There is not necessarily any need for a company experiencing trading difficulties to enter liquidation, although in the long term, this course of action may be thought preferable if it is felt that the desired financial performance of the company is unlikely ever to be achieved. In a period of recession, companies frequently take the decision to continue trading, mistakenly or otherwise, in the hope that future improvements in economic conditions will lead to improved trading results.

## Bankruptcy

Bankruptcy is a term which tends to be used loosely in connection with a company which has entered or is about to enter liquidation. In fact, in the UK, bankruptcy refers to the legal process whereby the assets of an insolvent individual – one who is unable to meet financial obligations to creditors – are distributed on a pro rata basis to creditors. To describe a company as 'bankrupt' is not accurate: a company in these circumstances is described as 'insolvent', and this is discussed below.

A petition for bankruptcy may be voluntary or it may be brought by a creditor. In the latter case, it will normally be the result of a demand for payment which is not satisfied, and if the payment is not subsequently made, it will be followed by a bankruptcy order. The debt must also be unsecured, and there must be a reasonable certainty that it will not be met.

It is less usual for bankruptcy to be voluntary, in that a debtor will normally try first to apply for an individual voluntary arrangement or IVA (see below). If creditors cannot agree to the terms of the IVA and believe they will obtain a larger proportion of the amounts owed to them via a bankruptcy arrangement, then the individual may have to present a petition for voluntary bankruptcy.

In most circumstances, first-time bankruptcy lasts for three years from the date the bankruptcy order is made, after which the bankrupt is automatically discharged. However, if the debtor has unsecured liabilities of less than £20,000 and has brought his or her own petition for bankruptcy, the discharge may occur after two years, and again is automatic. If it is a second or subsequent bankruptcy, the discharge is not automatic, and an individual will have to wait a minimum of five years before applying to the Court for a discharge.

One of the most serious issues arising for a bankrupt individual is that of the family home. The interests of a bankrupt's spouse carry some protection if the house is held in joint names, although a trustee (the practitioner who administers the bankrupt's affairs) can apply to the Court to dispose of the bankrupt's share of the property. The Court decision will take the following factors into account:

- the interests of creditors;
- the conduct of the spouse in relation to the bankruptcy;
- the financial needs and resources of the spouse;
- the needs of any children of the bankrupt;
- all circumstances other than the needs of the bankrupt.

These factors apply to a court application made in the first year after the trustee is appointed. After a year has elapsed, the interests of creditors take priority over all other factors, unless the circumstances are exceptional. The definition of 'exceptional' is not made clear by the Insolvency Act 1986, and the main aim of this clause appears to be the prevention of an absolute ruling regarding the sale of the family home.

The rationale for these provisions would appear to offer the bankrupt one year in which to satisfy payments to creditors by means other than the sale of the bankrupt's share of the family home. If this is not achieved within a year, it appears that the sale of the family home is regarded as a last resort to meet all or some of the bankrupt's debts.

## Individual voluntary arrangement (IVA)

As an alternative to bankruptcy, an individual may apply for an individual voluntary arrangement, or IVA, in order to satisfy outstanding payments to creditors, either in part or in whole. New provisions were introduced by the Insolvency Act 1986 to simplify the procedures for voluntary arrangements, which were previously covered by the Deeds of Arrangement Act of 1914. This still remains available, but has rarely been used.

In applying for an IVA, a proposal must be drawn up and presented to the Court setting out the reasons for the application, and why creditors should be satisfied with the proposed arrangement. It must include a statement of assets and liabilities, and proposals for dates and estimated amounts of payments to creditors. The aim of an IVA is to avoid the declaration of bankruptcy, and to realize assets to satisfy payments to creditors, probably on a pro-rata basis.

The advantage of an IVA is that the perceived stigma still attached to bankruptcy is avoided, because the individual is not declared bankrupt. Otherwise the results of the IVA are largely similar to a voluntary bankruptcy.

## Insolvency

Insolvency is the term used in the UK in connection with a company which is unable to meet its financial obligations to creditors. A distinction needs to be drawn between legal and technical insolvency, since the latter may be a temporary condition and would not necessarily require the company to be liquidated.

### Legal insolvency and liquidation

Legal insolvency refers to a situation where a company's total liabilities exceed its total assets so that the company is unable to satisfy its obligations to creditors and is unlikely to be in a position to do so in the future. One of two courses of action may result. First, a compulsory liquidation, or winding up by the court, can be instigated by petition by a creditor, providing that the outstanding debt exceeds £750.

Alternatively, voluntary liquidation can be initiated by the members of the company and may take the form of a members' voluntary liquidation or a creditors' voluntary liquidation. Although they are both set in action by the passing of a resolution by the company members, a members' voluntary liquidation is permitted only if the company can demonstrate that it will be able to pay its liabilities in full within twelve months of the commencement of the liquidation. If this is not the case, the process takes the form of a creditors' voluntary liquidation.

In both cases, the ultimate result of the liquidation is the termination of the legal existence of the company, which is 'dissolved'. The assets of the company are sold and the proceeds used to pay its creditors, following a strict order of priority. In the case of a compulsory winding up, it is likely that the cash realized from the sale of assets will be expended before the last category is reached. In the case of a voluntary winding up, this is less likely to be the case.

The procedures to be followed in a liquidation are complex, and involve the presentation of a petition in court, and the advertisement of this fact in the London Gazette.

It is also worth noting that the liquidation of a company does not necessarily result from its failure. There are circumstances where a perfectly healthy company is wound up, which include:

- the conversion of the company to an unincorporated entity such as a sole tradership or partnership;
- the restructuring of a group of companies, in which one or more of the group are liquidated;
- the decision to cease trading.

## Technical insolvency

Technical insolvency may not warrant the winding up of a company. Technical insolvency is generally said to occur when a company's current liabilities exceed its current assets. The company is therefore unable to meet its current financial obligations – although it may expect to be able to do so in the foreseeable future. A company may be technically insolvent and yet own substantial assets such as property, but if these are not immediately realizable, then this will have no impact on the company's ability to meet its current liabilities. The company will still have insufficient liquid resources – those which can readily be converted into cash – to pay its creditors. This may be a temporary condition and the company may still have unused sources of credit, but in the longer term it is often a warning sign of more serious future problems.

Conversely, it is worth noting that at the date at which audited accounts are prepared, a company's solvency position may appear healthy, with current assets exceeding current liabilities, so that sufficient liquid resources are immediately available to pay creditors. However, if a major source of credit is withdrawn at short notice, such as that from a major supplier of goods or a bank overdraft facility, technical and potentially legal insolvency may quickly result.

## Administrative receivership

The distinction between liquidation and receivership is often confused. A company may enter receivership without subsequently undergoing liquidation, although in practice this is often the case.

A receiver will usually be appointed to protect the interest in a company of a creditor, known as a debenture holder. A debenture holder is a third party who has a written acknowledgement of a debt due from the company. The debt may be secured by a fixed or floating charge over a company's assets, or it may be unsecured. A receiver may also be appointed by the Court, usually at the request of a secured creditor.

Legislation does not define the exact meaning of a debenture, but the definition is probably less important than the nature of the charge which is created over the company's assets, whether fixed or floating, or where no charge exists.

Unlike the process of liquidation, the aim of a receivership is to collect income from and / or to sell the charged assets of the company in order to satisfy the claim of the debenture holder. This may or may not involve the termination of the company's existence: in cases where a debenture holder has a floating charge over all the assets of the company, it may be more advantageous to continue the trading activities of the company with the aim of selling it as a going concern.

The receiver is bound to follow a strict order of priority in paying creditors, as follows:

1 Secured creditors with a fixed charge.
2 Preferential creditors, such as local and central government, and employees for pay arrears up to £800.
3 Secured creditors with a floating charge, usually including the debenture holders who appointed the receiver.
4 Special creditors such as finance houses and landlords.
5 Guaranteed creditors, such as employees for redundancy pay.

## Company administration

The office of administrator was introduced by the Insolvency Act 1986 to provide an alternative to liquidation for companies undergoing financial difficulties. An administrator may be appointed by the Court following petition by the company, its directors or a creditor, and often occurs where debenture holders are unwilling to appoint an administrative receiver.

The Court must be satisfied that the company is facing serious difficulties and that the appointment of an administrator is more advantageous to creditors than the winding up of the company. This means that there must be a reasonable expectation that the company can be returned to profitability, or that the administrator will realize a greater sum from the company's assets than if the company were liquidated. The outcome of the administration may be the survival or sale of the company, a voluntary arrangement with creditors or liquidation, depending on the administrator's findings and the decisions of creditors.

Once the petition has been presented to the Court, no separate action may be taken to wind up the company or to enforce any charge over the company's assets without the permission of the Court. If the Court does make the administration order, any other proceedings against the company are suspended unless Court permission is obtained, and any subsequent winding up petition will be dismissed while the order is in force.

A meeting of creditors must be held within three months of the appointment of the administrator at which the administrator's proposals for the company are discussed. It is important for creditors to attend the meeting as it is the only opportunity available to them to influence the administrator's proposals. If the administrator's proposals are not accepted by creditors, the Court will discharge the administration order. It is likely in this case that a separate action will subsequently be brought by creditors. If they are accepted, then the administrator will report this to the Court and take action to put the proposals into effect.

Company administration may be compared with an individual voluntary arrangement, in that the aim of the action in each case is to avoid either company liquidation or bankruptcy. In both cases, whether this is achieved depends to a large extent upon the attitudes of creditors of the company or individual in question.

## Statistics

The economic boom of the mid-1980s, when interest rates were relatively low and consumer spending levels high, provided a stimulus for the start-up of a large number of businesses. When economic conditions became less favourable in the late 1980s, many of these businesses, and particularly those which had remained small, were among the first to experience trading and financial difficulties. Indeed, research has shown that the age of a company is a significant factor in its potential for failure for the first five years of its existence.

While there has been an increase in company registrations in recent years, the growing trend in company liquidations in the same period provides sobering reading. Year on year, the absolute number of total insolvencies in England and Wales has been showing an increasing trend since 1988. The percentage of companies entering insolvency in terms of the total number of registered companies shows the same trend. In the last quarter of 1992, 2.2 per cent of total registered companies entered insolvency, whereas the percentage did not exceed 1.4 between 1987 and 1990.

The sharp increase in company insolvencies began in 1990, and the rise continued in 1991, reaching 45 per cent. Although the corresponding increase in 1992 was at a much lower level, at just

# Company Insolvencies in England and Wales

| Period | Compulsory Liquidations | Creditors' Voluntary Liquidations | Total Liquidations Quarterly | Total Liquidations Annually | % Variation Over Prior Year |
|---|---|---|---|---|---|
| **1987** | | | | | |
| Q1 | 1,131 | 2,096 | 3,227 | | |
| Q2 | 953 | 1,906 | 2,859 | | |
| Q3 | 694 | 1,859 | 2,553 | | |
| Q4 | 1,338 | 1,462 | 2,800 | 11,439 | |
| **1988** | | | | | |
| Q1 | 967 | 1,636 | 2,603 | | −19.3 |
| Q2 | 942 | 1,472 | 2,414 | | −15.6 |
| Q3 | 507 | 1,240 | 1,747 | | −31.6 |
| Q4 | 1,251 | 1,412 | 2,663 | 9,427 | − 4.9 |
| **1989** | | | | | |
| Q1 | 854 | 1,713 | 2,567 | | − 1.4 |
| Q2 | 1,103 | 1,711 | 2,814 | | 16.6 |
| Q3 | 548 | 1,479 | 2,027 | | 16.0 |
| Q4 | 1,515 | 1,533 | 3,048 | 10,456 | 14.5 |
| **1990** | | | | | |
| Q1 | 1,267 | 2,060 | 3,327 | | 29.6 |
| Q2 | 1,286 | 2,070 | 3,356 | | 19.3 |
| Q3 | 985 | 2,316 | 3,301 | | 62.9 |
| Q4 | 2,439 | 2,628 | 5,067 | 15,051 | 66.2 |
| **1991** | | | | | |
| Q1 | 2,076 | 3,364 | 5,440 | | 63.5 |
| Q2 | 2,155 | 3,460 | 5,615 | | 67.3 |
| Q3 | 1,368 | 3,332 | 4,700 | | 42.4 |
| Q4 | 2,769 | 3,303 | 6,072 | 21,827 | 19.8 |
| **1992** | | | | | |
| Q1 | 2,619 | 3,713 | 6,332 | | 16.4 |
| Q2 | 2,609 | 3,434 | 6,043 | | 7.6 |
| Q3 | 1,710 | 3,867 | 5,577 | | 18.7 |
| Q4 Est | 2,794 | 3,678 | 6,472 | 24,424 | 6.6 |

Source: Department of Trade and Industry

# Company Insolvencies in England and Wales
## Insolvencies by Industrial Sector

| INDUSTRY | 1987 | 1988 | 1989 | 1990 | 1991 | 1992 (to Q3) |
|---|---|---|---|---|---|---|
| Agriculture and horticulture | 126 | 73 | 78 | 111 | 135 | 141 |
| **Manufacturing** | | | | | | |
| Food, drink & tobacco | 140 | 88 | 105 | 109 | 171 | 149 |
| Chemicals | 97 | 75 | 85 | 97 | 134 | 90 |
| Metals & engineering | 1,035 | 708 | 697 | 972 | 1,344 | 1,183 |
| Textiles & clothing | 1,041 | 811 | 959 | 921 | 1,052 | 851 |
| Timber & furniture | 378 | 242 | 302 | 391 | 527 | 382 |
| Paper, printing & publishing | 380 | 326 | 425 | 552 | 856 | 628 |
| Other | 557 | 480 | 468 | 792 | 939 | 746 |
| Sub-total | **3,628** | **2,730** | **3,041** | **3,834** | **5,023** | **4,029** |
| Construction | 1,490 | 1,471 | 1,638 | 2,445 | 3,373 | 2,851 |
| Transport & communication | 657 | 548 | 589 | 932 | 1,246 | 937 |
| Sub-total | **2,147** | **2,019** | **2,227** | **3,377** | **4,619** | **3,788** |
| **Wholesaling** | | | | | | |
| Food, drink & tobacco | 238 | 125 | 162 | 235 | 287 | 300 |
| Motor vehicles | 134 | 91 | 69 | 107 | 152 | 144 |
| Other | 511 | 487 | 428 | 724 | 841 | 494 |
| Sub-total | **883** | **703** | **659** | **1,066** | **1,280** | **938** |
| **Retailing** | | | | | | |
| Food, drink & tobacco | 216 | 170 | 165 | 244 | 291 | 305 |
| Motor vehicles & filling stations | 173 | 121 | 136 | 174 | 245 | 223 |
| Other | 1,047 | 795 | 738 | 1,181 | 1,578 | 1,285 |
| Sub-total | **1,436** | **1,086** | **1,039** | **1,599** | **2,114** | **1,813** |
| Financial institutions | 212 | 159 | 167 | 303 | 394 | 379 |
| Business services | 781 | 843 | 952 | 1,558 | 2,396 | 2,095 |
| Hotels & catering | 380 | 359 | 371 | 489 | 748 | 767 |
| Other | 1,846 | 1,455 | 1,922 | 2,714 | 5,118 | 4,002 |
| Sub-total | **3,219** | **2,816** | **3,412** | **5,064** | **8,656** | **7,243** |
| **Total** | **11,439** | **9,427** | **10,456** | **15,051** | **21,827** | **17,952** |

Source: Department of Trade & Industry

under 12 per cent, the actual number of insolvencies had never-theless grown to a record 24,424. It had been hoped that the reduction in the bank base rate to 10 per cent in May 1992, followed by further reductions later that year, should help ease the burden for companies of interest charges on bank borrowings and stimulate consumer spending. There is as yet little evidence to show whether the projected improvement in economic con-ditions and increased consumer demand will take place in time to help the large number of companies which have wavered between survival and failure in recent years.

The failure problem is clearly concentrated within smaller and medium-sized businesses, the vast majority of which do not receive attention in the media except as statistics. In spite of this, the number of individuals associated with these businesses who have suffered serious financial loss and the resulting distress this causes is enormous. However, larger and quoted companies are suffering as well, in terms of maintaining turnover and profit margins, and the implications for their workforces are particu-larly gloomy. The number of redundancies announced from companies such as Ford, British Aerospace and Vickers through-out the second half of 1992 is a worrying indicator of expectations for the short- and medium-term future.

## Company insolvencies

The insolvency problem is not contained within any particular industrial sector, although one of the worst affected is arguably the construction industry. After the peak in house prices in 1988 / 1989, the collapse which followed in 1989 as the bank base rate was pushed to 15 per cent was not surprising, although highly damaging to those who believed the bubble could not burst.

Insolvencies in the construction industry reached their highest level in absolute terms in 1992, with, 2,851 companies failing in the first nine months of the year. This gloomy picture is borne out by the Chairman of the residential property development group, John Maunders Group plc, who says in his 1991 statement to the accounts: 'It had been expected that reducing interest rates would have helped the Industry out of recession but this anticipated improvement has been offset by rising unemployment and a continuing lack of purchaser confidence.' Indeed, his words could be applied to most industrial sectors in both 1991 and 1992.

Bett Brothers plc, the building and property development group, suffered a loss in 1991 for the first time in their forty-five-year history, amounting to £9.2 million after tax and dividends. Although they enjoyed an increase in turnover, gross margins declined from 38 per cent in 1990 to 17 per cent in 1991. Their Chairman describes the reasons for the loss as 'almost entirely due to our exposure in the depressed South and South East of England property market', although he points out that 'the Board has been quick in taking action to ensure that, as far as possible, there will be no repetition of these losses'. Many of the smaller companies associated with the construction industry, however, will not be in a position to outlive the depression in the property market.

The business services market is also facing a large increase in numbers of insolvencies. This sector has seen rises of 64 per cent and 54 per cent in 1990 and 1991 respectively, with numbers increasing from 952 in 1989 to 2,396 in 1991. With over 2,000 insolvencies in the first nine months of 1992 alone, the upward trend is continuing.

It is clear that severe problems are emerging in the retailing sector as well. The Asda Group plc, for example, suffered a decline in its operating margin of some 2 per cent in 1992, which in monetary terms translates to some £82.4 million. As the Chairman comments in his annual statement, 'Results for the year are clearly unsatisfactory.' It was also a year in which staff received no salary increases, a drastic way of cutting operating costs.

The case of Dan-Air illustrates how widespread the effects of failure of a substantial business concern can be. Negotiations with British Airways for the latter to take over Dan-Air attracted criticism in terms of the reduction in competition in the airline industry. It was argued that it would have been more advantageous for consumers if Dan-Air had been liquidated in order to promote increased competition between the remaining airlines.

On the other hand, it could be argued that the takeover option is preferable for employees, creditors and travellers, in that more jobs would be saved, redundancy packages would be more favourable, trade creditors would receive a greater degree of protection and consumers would not suffer disruption of their travel plans. The arguments against the takeover carry some weight, but for those likely to suffer financial loss from the failure, it may quite understandably be considered the safer option.

Although the potential effects of failure or decline in these larger companies are widespread and serious, they do have a better chance than smaller companies of negotiating rescue packages. The end of smaller companies tends to be swift and final.

The case of a medium-sized transport company operating in the South East illustrates this. The company delivered mens' clothing to three major High Street retailers, enjoyed a constant flow of work and appeared to exercise effective control over their overhead expenditure. However, no reliable accounting or costing records were maintained; sales prices, for example, were determined simply by undercutting competitors' prices. Disaster began when a customer was lost to a competitor, representing a loss of some 30 per cent of turnover. Because the company operated in such a specialized area, it proved impossible to win new customers in the short term.

The company finally collapsed following a VAT inspection: it had paid only estimated assessments from HM Customs and Excise rather than attempting to complete VAT returns from scant records. A large VAT liability was discovered which the company was unable to pay. Their bankers refused additional support because the quality of management information was so poor that the company was considered a bad risk. The only solution, ultimately, was liquidation. Personal bank guarantees also forced the sale of the Managing Director's house, and effectively his financial ruin. Reliance on too small a customer base and a complete lack of management information were the two major factors which caused the company's demise; these could have been avoided.

# Individual Insolvencies in England and Wales

| Period | Bankruptcy Orders | Individual Voluntary Arrangements | Total Insolvencies Quarterly | Total Insolvencies Annually | % Variation Over Prior Year |
|---|---|---|---|---|---|
| 1987 | | | | | |
| Q1 | 1,721 | 55 | 1,776 | | |
| Q2 | 1,820 | 101 | 1,921 | | |
| Q3 | 1,687 | 115 | 1,802 | | |
| Q4 | 1,766 | 162 | 1,928 | 7,427 | |
| 1988 | | | | | |
| Q1 | 2,092 | 184 | 2,276 | | 28.2 |
| Q2 | 2,025 | 187 | 2,212 | | 15.2 |
| Q3 | 1,695 | 221 | 1,916 | | 6.3 |
| Q4 | 1,905 | 198 | 2,103 | 8,507 | 9.1 |
| 1989 | | | | | |
| Q1 | 1,972 | 252 | 2,224 | | − 2.3 |
| Q2 | 2,103 | 315 | 2,418 | | 9.3 |
| Q3 | 1,837 | 322 | 2,159 | | 12.7 |
| Q4 | 2,226 | 338 | 2,564 | 9,365 | 22.0 |
| 1990 | | | | | |
| Q1 | 2,514 | 428 | 2,942 | | 32.3 |
| Q2 | 2,804 | 424 | 3,228 | | 33.5 |
| Q3 | 3,018 | 529 | 3,547 | | 64.3 |
| Q4 | 3,722 | 548 | 4,270 | 13,987 | 66.5 |
| 1991 | | | | | |
| Q1 | 4,835 | 601 | 5,436 | | 84.8 |
| Q2 | 5,337 | 721 | 6,058 | | 87.7 |
| Q3 | 5,523 | 862 | 6,385 | | 80.0 |
| Q4 | 6,937 | 824 | 7,761 | 25,640 | 81.8 |
| 1992 | | | | | |
| Q1 | 8,389 | 992 | 9,381 | | 72.6 |
| Q2 | 7,791 | 1,217 | 9,008 | | 48.7 |
| Q3 | 7,506 | 1,253 | 8,759 | | 37.2 |
| Q4 Est | 8,420 | 1,226 | 9,646 | 36,794 | 24.3 |

Note: Individual voluntary arrangements include deeds of arrangement

Source: Department of Trade and Industry

## Bankruptcy Orders and Deeds of Arrangement in England and Wales
## Analysis by Industrial Sector

| INDUSTRY | 1987 | 1988 | 1989 | 1990 | 1991 | 1992 (to Q3) |
|---|---|---|---|---|---|---|
| *Agriculture and horticulture* | 172 | 162 | 142 | 198 | 266 | 240 |
| **Manufacturing** | | | | | | |
| *Food, drink & tobacco* | 17 | 25 | 9 | 31 | 48 | 46 |
| *Chemicals* | 2 | 3 | 3 | 4 | 12 | 7 |
| *Metals & engineering* | 147 | 158 | 180 | 240 | 424 | 468 |
| *Textiles & clothing* | 63 | 73 | 77 | 63 | 152 | 135 |
| *Timber & furniture* | 83 | 94 | 62 | 116 | 233 | 251 |
| *Paper, printing & publishing* | 39 | 60 | 39 | 80 | 143 | 152 |
| *Other* | 35 | 30 | 38 | 67 | 120 | 91 |
| *Sub-total* | **386** | **443** | **408** | **601** | **1,132** | **1,150** |
| *Construction* | 1,123 | 1,590 | 1,652 | 2,348 | 3,812 | 3,515 |
| *Transport & communication* | 464 | 527 | 601 | 953 | 1,620 | 1,542 |
| *Sub-total* | **1,587** | **2,117** | **2,253** | **3,301** | **5,432** | **5,057** |
| **Wholesaling** | | | | | | |
| *Food, drink & tobacco* | 45 | 53 | 42 | 57 | 68 | 82 |
| *Motor vehicles* | 0 | 6 | 4 | 8 | 21 | 39 |
| *Other* | 61 | 69 | 67 | 81 | 122 | 141 |
| *Sub-total* | **106** | **128** | **113** | **146** | **211** | **262** |
| **Retailing** | | | | | | |
| *Food, drink & tobacco* | 468 | 447 | 401 | 595 | 895 | 767 |
| *Motor vehicles & filling stations* | 138 | 163 | 131 | 155 | 362 | 277 |
| *Other* | 620 | 459 | 491 | 807 | 1,442 | 1,619 |
| *Sub-total* | **1,226** | **1,069** | **1,023** | **1,557** | **2,699** | **2,663** |
| *Financial institutions* | 99 | 86 | 95 | 143 | 247 | 194 |
| *Business services* | 486 | 325 | 386 | 662 | 1,284 | 1,350 |
| *Hotels & catering* | 594 | 625 | 719 | 867 | 1,481 | 1,722 |
| *Other* | 462 | 646 | 724 | 1,014 | 1,857 | 1,893 |
| *Sub-total* | **1,641** | **1,682** | **1,924** | **2,686** | **4,869** | **5,159** |
| **Total self-employed individuals** | **5,118** | **5,601** | **5,863** | **8,489** | **14,609** | **14,531** |

| Other Individuals | | | | | | |
|---|---|---|---|---|---|---|
| *Employees* | 591 | 686 | 856 | 1,172 | 1,639 | 1,838 |
| *No occupation/unemployed* | 597 | 652 | 698 | 1,107 | 2,811 | 3,309 |
| *Directors/promoters of companies* | 441 | 345 | 305 | 427 | 667 | 713 |
| *Occupation unknown* | 276 | 444 | 419 | 865 | 2,906 | 3,295 |
| *Sub-total other individuals* | **1,905** | **2,127** | **2,278** | **3,571** | **8,023** | **9,155** |
| **Total orders/deeds of arrangement** | **7,023** | **7,728** | **8,141** | **12,060** | **22,632** | **23,686** |

Note: From 1991 deeds of arrangement not included. IVAs excluded in all years.

Source: Department of Trade & Industry

Although small and medium-sized businesses are to a degree at the mercy of the strength of the economy, careful planning, control and communication are essential if they are to maximize their chances of survival.

Levels of individual insolvencies show a trend broadly similar to that for companies for the past five years, although the increases between 1990 and 1992 are still more marked. The increases in absolute terms from 13,987 in 1990 to 25,640 and 36,794 in 1991 and 1992 respectively represent rises of over 83 per cent and 43 per cent. In spite of dramatic drops in both bank base rates and the level of inflation, some analysts are arguing that these levels are likely to continue rising throughout 1993, as the lack of a significant perceived improvement in economic activity claims still more victims of past high interest rates and dampened consumer demand.

As in the case of company insolvencies, a sharp increase in individual bankruptcies in absolute terms appears in the construction industry, which also makes the largest contribution to total bankruptcies in every year from 1987 to 1992.

The contribution made to total bankruptcies by the manufacturing, wholesaling, retailing and service sectors remains surprisingly static throughout the five-year period. However, in each sector, there is a marked percentage increase in both the 1990 and 1991 level of bankruptcies compared with prior years. In 1991, these increases range from 44.5 per cent in the wholesaling sector to over 88 per cent in manufacturing industries. Although the rises level out slightly in 1992, the actual numbers of bankruptcies and voluntary arrangements are still increasing, bringing no respite in the financial and associated emotional distress for the individuals involved.

As with smaller companies, the chances of rescue for individuals tend to be limited, and the effects of failure devastating for those involved. The experience of a stationery supplier is a case in point. Operating in a small town in the South East, this sole trader had used his excellent sales skills to gain the custom of a significant proportion of the small businesses in the surrounding area. Although individual sales were largely of low value, they were of a steadily increasing volume. Perhaps for this reason, together with a lack of accounting information, debt collection was a major problem, and outstanding amounts gradually increased until the business was suffering severe cashflow problems. To stem the increasing bank overdraft, payments to creditors were stalled, until suppliers lost patience and withdrew their trade credit terms.

As difficulties in obtaining supplies increased, so customers lost patience with the long delays in the delivery of basic items – and turned to alternative sources for their stationery supplies. Within a short period of time the business collapsed completely. Although the amounts it owed to creditors were relatively small, the proprietor was required to wind up the business via an individual voluntary arrangement and to sell his house to meet these liabilities. This is a sad case of a person who operates extremely well in his own field, but lacks experience in running a business effectively. Improved record-keeping and a more vigorous approach to debt-collection would probably have saved the business if these problems had been recognized early enough; but all chances of additional financial support had disappeared by the time this happened.

However, some failures and bankruptcies stem from factors which are beyond the control of individuals. This has become particularly evident in the construction industry where many small businesses and individuals work on a sub-contract basis. In major construction projects, there may be a chain of sub-contractors, all of whom will pay their own creditors only when they have been paid themselves. The implications for those at the end of the chain when a project is suspended are ruinous, and mean (for many) that basic expenditure such as mortgage repayments cannot be met. This has become a particular problem at a time when the construction industry has been in decline for a long period.

A skilled electrician became a victim of this type of problem while working on an office project in a large city. He had initially been delighted to be involved in the project, since it represented several months' work at a time when competition was becoming increasingly stiff. However, the business for which he was sub-contracting ran into difficulties after another of its main projects was suspended. The business was owed considerable sums of money, and found itself unable to pay its own sub-contractors. For this electrician, these events spelt disaster, at least in the short-term: he had relied on this project and had deliberately not sought any other work in the meantime. He could not have foreseen the suspension of the project or the resulting chain of events, but this fact did not provide any comfort in financial terms at a time when work was becoming increasingly difficult to find.

All of these statistics and experiences present a dismal picture for companies and individuals in business alike and the prospects for the immediate, if not the medium-term, future are less than encouraging, especially for those individuals whose small businesses have struggled to survive so far.

## Financial implications of insolvency

An area less commonly discussed in relation to business failure statistics is the number of associated individuals and businesses affected by failure. When a company or individual becomes insolvent, and in particular where a company liquidation results, various groups of people both outside and within the company will be directly affected. Those outside the company will include suppliers, providers of finance and customers, and within the company, employees, management and shareholders. The knock-on effects of a single business failure represent a loss of income, whether large or small, for all of these groups. There are also specific and serious implications for company directors, which are discussed separately below.

## Suppliers and providers of finance

In many cases, liquidation or bankruptcy proceedings will be initiated by a creditor, who may be either a supplier of goods or services to the company, or a provider of finance. Depending on the status of the creditor, there may be an immediate loss in terms of the cash owed by the company or individual, either in part or in whole. The creditor also stands to lose a source of profits as a result of the liquidation, either in the form of the margins charged on goods sold or interest charged on finance provided.

In the case of individual bankruptcies, where the debtor brings a petition for an individual voluntary arrangement, creditors may initially be reluctant to offer their consent to the arrangement. This is likely to be the case if the creditor ranks well down the list in the priority of payments, and feels there is a greater chance of payment if trading continues.

## Customers

The problems of customers where a company or individual becomes insolvent are less obvious, but may be no less considerable. If a customer has paid in advance for a product or service which they have not yet received, they may have little chance of recovering their money. Alternatively, they may be left with a partially completed project which is of no use in its incomplete state.

The case of the Bank of Credit and Commerce International in 1991 provides a dramatic illustration of the effects on customers of the downfall of a business, where the impact on the public is significant.

## Employees

One of the most difficult tasks faced by a liquidator is breaking the news of a company liquidation to its employees – a task the management of a company often feel unable to undertake. Employees are likely to be the persons hardest hit by a liquidation, in spite of the provision of a degree of financial protection offered by redundancy payments. Particularly where someone has held a specialized or comparatively unskilled post for a considerable number of years, the opportunities for employment elsewhere may be severely limited. Where the company represents a major employer in a relatively small community, the implications for the entire community may be very serious.

### Management and shareholders

Again, for management and especially those in middle-management posts and of middle age, the implications of a company ceasing to exist may be long term and the prospects of finding a similar post quickly slim. In a small company, the shareholders are often also those who manage the company and liquidation can represent the loss of all income for these people.

## Statutory implications of insolvency

The possibility of a company becoming insolvent and entering liquidation has serious statutory implications for two further parties in particular – directors and auditors.

### Directors

Directors need to be aware of their statutory responsibilities where there is any possibility that a company may go into insolvent liquidation, either compulsory or voluntary. In certain circumstances, under the provisions of the 1986 Directors Disqualification Act, directors can be disqualified from holding directorships for a period usually between two and fifteen years and / or made to contribute personally to the assets of the company. The period of disqualification will depend largely on the conduct of a director in the period leading up to the liquidation, and the extent of any involvement in previous insolvencies. One of the purposes of the measures contained within both the Directors Disqualification Act and the Insolvency Act 1986 regarding directors is to try to promote improved standards of company management, and to ensure that directors adequately fulfil their duties and responsibilities.

In periods of adverse economic conditions, the role of a director actively involved in the day-to-day operations of a company becomes a particularly difficult one. A conflict may well arise between a desire to avoid the failure of a declining business and an awareness of the seriousness of the potential consequences if the company does subsequently fail.

If a company does become insolvent, the person subsequently responsible for handling the company (such as the liquidator or administrative receiver) is required to assess the performance of the directors of the company in the three years prior to insolvency. A director may be judged to be unfit to be involved in the management of a company under the provisions of the Directors Disqualification Act or guilty of 'wrongful trading' as defined by the Insolvency Act. Additionally, an 'aggrieved person' – perhaps a supplier or customer of the company – who believes they have evidence of a director's unfitness should notify the liquidator or receiver as soon as possible.

Specific issues which may be considered in assessing the conduct of directors include:

- breach of duty or misapplication of funds or property of the company.
- initiating transactions which defraud creditors or other parties.
- failure by the company to provide goods or services to customers which have been paid for, either wholly or in part.
- failure to keep proper accounting records and to file appropriate documents and accounts.

Wrongful trading is established by reference to three criteria:

- the company has entered insolvent liquidation, that is, it has gone into liquidation and is unable to meet payments to creditors and winding up expenses from the cash realized from the sale of its assets.
- the director was aware, or ought to have been aware, before the company entered insolvent liquidation, that it had no reasonable prospect of avoiding doing so.
- the individual was a director at the time.

A director cannot escape these responsibilities by resigning after he or she was aware, or ought to have been aware, that there was little reasonable prospect that the company would avoid entering insolvent liquidation. However, if he or she can satisfy the Court that every step was taken to minimize the potential losses to creditors of the company, in the knowledge that the company was likely to enter liquidation, then it may be possible to avoid liability. Ignorance will not be accepted as a defence.

Directors are also expected to take steps to ensure that the losses suffered by creditors of the company are minimized, where there is a reasonable possibility that the company will be liquidated on the grounds of insolvency. These might include ceasing to order goods on credit, and even ceasing trading where it is felt to be appropriate.

Clearly, the responsibilities of holding the office of company director are not to be taken lightly. If a director feels a potential problem exists within his or her company, the first step is to contact an insolvency practitioner without delay to discuss the specific circumstances.

It is also worth noting that small businesses which cannot afford the services of a solicitor might qualify to use the 'Lawyers For Enterprise' scheme, by which businesses receive a free consultation with a solicitor. Details of participating solicitors are held by the Law Society.

## Auditors

Auditors cannot be made to contribute to the assets of a company which has entered insolvent liquidation. However, they are expected to comment in their annual audit report to the members of the company if it is judged that there are doubts as to the company's status as a going concern.

The question of going concern is arguably one of the most difficult issues upon which the auditor has to express an opinion, and for which little guidance has been offered in the past by Statements of Standard Accounting Practice. The auditor is expected to judge from the balance sheet and profit and loss account whether there is a reasonable prospect that the company will be unable to continue its operations in the foreseeable future. Reliance must therefore be placed on knowledge of the company and industry in question and past experience in making the subjective decision whether to qualify a company's audit report on the grounds of going concern.

In December 1991, the Auditing Practices Board announced its proposal to change audit reporting practice to expand the information value of audit reports. This will include more detailed reporting requirements for fundamental issues such as going concern. The proposed Standard states that attention should be drawn to 'inherent uncertainties' where the validity of the going concern assumption is affected.

If the Statement is adopted, it will require auditors to take a more active role in the assessment of potential business failure, by carrying out procedures which are specifically designed to assess whether the going concern basis of preparation of the financial statements is appropriate.

First, auditors will be required to obtain a written statement from the directors of the company backed up by appropriate documentary evidence that the company is a going concern. This statement must be made with specific reference to events which are expected to occur within one year of having signed off the financial statements and thereafter. The appropriate evidence is likely to include forecasts and budgets prepared by the company together with supporting bases and assumptions and statements of borrowing facilities available to the company.

If, as a result of their work, auditors believe there are uncertainties which adversely affect the company's ability to continue as a going concern, they should consider whether these matters are adequately disclosed in the financial statements. If this is not the case, then a qualification to this effect should be included in the auditors' report. Even where disclosure is adequate, attention should be drawn to these matters in the report.

The benefits of such disclosure should be twofold. First, users of financial statements often do not have the expertise to detect and analyse potential financial problems and risks faced by a company from the information contained within financial statements. Any additional information which helps users to reach informed decisions regarding, for example, their investment in a company is to be welcomed.

Second, the responsibility placed on directors to give specific consideration to future circumstances which may affect the company's viability as a going concern emphasizes the need for companies to plan ahead effectively. Although the information provided by directors is subject to scrutiny by auditors, the fact that provision of such information is likely to become a statutory requirement must ultimately benefit companies in focusing attention on future events.

At best, this is a sensitive area. At worst it can lead to extremely costly claims for negligence against auditors who have signed a 'clean' audit report for a company which is later liquidated on the grounds of insolvency. On the other hand, many companies are unwilling to accept the need for a going concern qualification to appear in their audit report, given the potential damage which might result to the company's reputation as a successful trading entity. In view of recent years' rises in both company and individual insolvencies, the proposed changes to expand the information value of financial statements should provide benefits to all users of a company's financial statements. Whether the changes will also increase the practical problems of auditors in reporting upon the financial affairs of a company remains to be seen.

# 2. Characteristics of failing businesses

The final descent of a business towards collapse is often hastened by poor management of business factors which it may be possible to remedy or avoid if they are recognized and preventative action taken soon enough. These factors may or may not be overtly concerned with the financial management of a business, but they will inevitably impact on its financial performance and stability.

Business failures are generally analysed from a quantitative rather than a qualitative viewpoint: their financial characteristics are scrutinized rather than behavioural features or errors in management. This is no surprise, since after the event, it is the financial impact of the failure which is of greatest concern to affected parties, not the reasons for the downfall of the business. Qualitative analysis cannot offer a cure for a failing business, but it can provide useful indicators of types of business behaviour which will hasten failure.

John Argenti, who has written various works on aspects of business management and is established as an authority on corporate collapse, was among the first analysts to make an extensive study of the specific issues which can lead a company into failure. As he points out, the diagnosis of decline is by no means clear cut, and there usually exists a combination of factors which will finally push a business over the brink into failure.

It may not be immediately obvious to the business owner or manager how this can be used to the benefit of their business. In a practical sense, the most important point is for those in control of a business to become aware of the type of problem that can be most destructive. This chapter tries to illustrate this by looking at examples of companies which have collapsed or been in danger of doing so.

In his study of the causes and symptoms of business failure,

John Argenti identified three predominant paths followed by a declining business, where a reasonably easily identifiable pattern of performance can be observed. In simple terms these 'types' can be described as:

- 'Never should have existed'
- 'Has been'
- 'Slow death'.

The negative factors which contribute to the eventual failure of businesses which fall into the three categories are varied, but there are certain issues which arise repeatedly. Argenti enumerated the factors which proved most significant, and some of these and others are discussed later in this chapter.

It is also important to remember that in periods of poor economic conditions, additional demands in the form of long periods of high interest rates and reduced consumer demand, for example, are placed on businesses – and especially impact on small ones. The definition of a small business can be a tricky one: according to, say, the Companies Act, a small company is one which satisfies two of the following three criteria:

- it has less than 50 employees;
- turnover does not exceed £2.8 million;
- the balance sheet total does not exceed £1.4 million.

However, many of the businesses which are most at risk probably fall well below these limits. It is likely that some which otherwise might have survived in better conditions will find themselves in serious decline. Whether it remains justifiable to attach the above labels to certain businesses under these conditions is arguable, but it is generally true that the paths of business performance which characterize the three types will still be observable, and if anything the effects will be more prominent.

One of the important assumptions made by Argenti in his analysis is that whatever the prevailing economic conditions, there will always be a certain number of business failures every year which can be perceived as a natural 'fall-out'. In some cases it may be that failure is not necessarily a fate to be avoided at all costs, but rather that if it is inevitable, action should be taken to minimize its effects. This premise becomes more complex when trading and economic conditions are difficult, and the proportion of businesses whose demise is aggravated by external factors is likely to be higher.

Argenti's assumption about a natural fall-out also brings out the point that even when economic recession comes to an end, and confidence is generally improving, businesses can still fall prey to the problems which lead to failure. Economic pressures may become less severe, but normal business hazards and problems must still be contended with.

The other significant assumption made by Argenti in describing the three trajectories is that no change in management occurs during the trading period in question. A change in management can make the difference between survival and failure.

As might be expected, the three trajectories display contrasting paths, and tend to extend over differing periods of time.

## Type 1 failure: 'Never should have existed'

Type 1 failure is the category into which many small and declining businesses fall. The label 'Never should have existed' might be attached to these businesses on the grounds that, if detailed planning had been carried out and properly assessed, the business might well not have been established. Performance in broad terms tends not to improve beyond 'poor' throughout the existence of the business, and this existence usually proves to be short lived.

From the start, the business often falls prey to an array of management defects which will ultimately manifest themselves as both the symptoms and causes of its failure. Small businesses of this type also frequently suffer shortcomings in their accounting systems and financial management, and cashflow is likely to be a severe constraint.

These defects are very rarely the result of wilful mismanagement, but tend to result from inexperience and lack of expertise in detecting potential problem areas in the business. What is most important in these cases is to recognize problem areas early on and to take appropriate action to remedy or limit them. For a smaller business, this will include making best use of available sources of advice, ranging from local Enterprise Agencies to a good accountant who takes a positive interest in helping to guide the business through its early stages.

It is not really possible to compile a list of the factors which most commonly contribute to Type 1 failures, but a number of issues which frequently arise are covered later in this chapter. One of the most common danger signs in a small failing business is a chronic shortage of cash. It need not be a large shortfall, but sufficient to ensure that management of the bank account is a constant juggling process. A shortage of cash is not in itself a cause of failure: it is the management of cash resources which is the real problem. This area is examined in more detail in chapter 5.

Illustrations of well-known cases which fall into the Type 1 failure category are less easily found than those which fall into the other two categories. One of the main reasons for this is that these businesses tend to have a short life span, and understandably do not often achieve a particularly high public profile. However, a slightly unusual example can be found in Data Magnetics, a company which lasted only three years and whose demise did not, in fact, result from either financial or technical inexperience or lack of expertise.*

## DATA MAGNETICS

The company was set up in response to a perceived gap in the high technology market of thin film disk manufacture, for use in the production of computer hard disk drives, then widely

---

* A more detailed description and analysis of this and other companies used as case studies in this chapter can be found in *The Phoenix Factor – Lessons for Success from Management Failure* by David Clutterbuck and Sue Kernaghan, and *Turnaround – How twenty well-known companies came back from the brink*, edited by Rebecca Nelson with David Clutterbuck. See *Further reading* for publication details.

known as 'Winchester' disk drives. There were no manufacturers of these disks in the UK, or indeed in Europe. Given
the problems associated with the long-distance purchase of a
high technology product from suppliers in the USA and
Japan, it was felt that Data Magnetics would be assured of a
significant market share in Europe. Additionally, the technology itself was advancing. Data Magnetics believed that the
company would be able to perfect this technology, and that
being the first to do so would give them an additional
competitive edge.

One of the main dangers in high technology markets is the
unpredictability both of future market requirements and of
the duration of the research processes required to satisfy those
requirements. Delays in the development of new products can
mean that they are in fact outdated before the technology is
perfected, or that other developments have occurred which
remove the need for the product altogether.

A major problem experienced by Data Magnetics was raising
the start-up capital required by the project, which took far longer
than had been anticipated. The same was true of the development of the technology. It had been estimated that fifteen to
eighteen months of research would be required before
production began on a large scale. In fact, a combination of
setbacks including new, competing technology, a need for
further investment and difficulties in the manufacture of a
consistently perfect product in high volumes meant that forecast
levels of income simply could not be generated within the
expected timescale.

Eventually, throughout 1988, Data Magnetics succeeded in
overcoming the technical difficulties which had delayed
production. However, it proved to be too late, even though it
was estimated that the company would break even that year.
Additional investment would still be required to ensure the
success of the business, and investors were not prepared to add
to the £14 million which had already been sunk in the
company. The result was that the company was left with
insufficient financial resources to provide adequate working
capital or to fund a continuing development programme.

It had taken longer than anticipated to raise the venture capital required to finance Data Magnetics, and the company survived only a further three years before an administrative receiver was called in. Months later, the company was sold to an Israeli consortium.

Whether Data Magnetics was strictly a company which 'Never should have existed' is open to question. The initiative for the formation of the company came from 3i, the venture capitalists, who had identified the gap in the market and supplied the concept for the company from its contact with a disk drive manufacturer. The management and technical team were experienced and highly competent, but were unable to contend with the combination of unforeseen problems which plagued the company throughout its existence.

The case of Data Magnetics does, however, illustrate the difficulties associated with operating in such a high technology sector where the needs of industry change constantly, and where the timescale for the development of products to satisfy those needs cannot be forecast with accuracy. In this sense, it is a high-risk market, and also one which requires intensive investment in terms of both finance and time.

Could the failure have been avoided? In the final year before the company was put into receivership, it was believed that the technical problems associated with its product had been overcome, and that success in financial terms would follow. However, in cases such as this where substantial external support is required at the inception of the business, investors are understandably concerned for the safety of their investment and do expect to see some return. Once confidence in the business begins to deteriorate, it is extremely difficult to regenerate it unless very tangible signs of success manifest themselves. For Data Magnetics, this could not be achieved and support was withdrawn.

This can be compared with many cases of small businesses whose bankers withdraw overdraft facilities just when its owners believe that success is around the corner.

# Type 2 failure: 'Has been'

Type 2 failures as described by Argenti tend to be more spectacular in their business performance, both in success and failure, and usually have a longer lifespan than Type 1 failures.

The successful period of performance in businesses of this type is often due to an outstanding personality, who demonstrates high-powered selling skills, driving ambition, singlemindedness and absolute confidence both in self and the business. Within a few years of the commencement of the business, the product and personality have combined to ensure that sales, profits and the financial stability of the company are improving, often at an astonishing rate. In some cases, this success will have attracted media attention, and the need to succeed becomes even more pressing as a result. The downfall of such businesses can be equally spectacular: turnover continues to grow, but is not matched by profits. The actual stability of the business proves to be considerably less than appeared to be the case, and, given its high profile, decline can occur extremely swiftly as confidence in the business ebbs and support is withdrawn.

It should be mentioned that this type of failure is the least common, although businesses falling into this category may attract considerable attention.

### SINCLAIR RESEARCH

Sinclair Research is a good example of a Type 2 failure. The business was based on Sinclair's ability to discern a niche in the high street technology market and to use his innovative – rather than business – skills to attempt to satisfy it. His first business, Sinclair Radionics, was set up in 1962, and in 1972 brought out the first pocket calculator based on a single chip. He was also the first to launch scientific and programmable calculators, and three years later the world's first digital watch.

Sinclair clearly caught the imagination of consumers, in creating products which were cheap but exciting, but these were lacking in one important area – quality and durability. It was discovered, for example, that the lifespan of his original digital watch batteries was only a matter of days. Sinclair had succeeded in taking the first steps towards winning a substantial market share in high-tech products and had attracted a good deal of media attention, but he was unable to sustain this initial success by satisfying his market in the longer term.

By 1979, Sinclair Radionics had failed as a business. After his opening success in the pocket calculator market, Sinclair had used his profits to fund research for further new products. Japanese manufacturers on the other hand had been perfecting the basic pocket calculator technology, to produce a range of products which were both cheap and reliable. Eventually of course, it was these Japanese manufacturers whose products were in demand.

However, Sinclair set up a new business, Sinclair Research, and in 1980 launched the first home computer. For the next three years, Sinclair was the market leader in the home computer market, its sales and profitability outstripping rivals such as Amstrad and Dragon. Once again Sinclair had caught the imagination of the consumer, and although technical problems with his computers did exist, their effects were mitigated by a 'No questions asked' exchange policy which no rival could match.

Again, Sinclair was not satisfied by building up existing markets, but continually forged ahead with newer and more sophisticated technology. Although competitors such as Amstrad and Commodore were fighting to build up their market share, Sinclair retained the lead until Christmas 1984, when disastrous sales levels left the business with vast quantities of unsold computers – and mounting debts.

The final disaster occurred in the form of the C5, the electronically powered vehicle. Although this project was financed by Sinclair personally, it dealt a blow to his reputation as a serious innovator, although he clearly believed there was a demand for such a vehicle. The cash problems experienced by Sinclair Research had not abated, and eventually in 1986 after various offers of rescue packages and rescheduling of debt repayments, the computer business was sold to Alan Sugar of Amstrad for £5 million. This increased Amstrad's market share to some 85 per cent, placing Amstrad in an extremely powerful position. However, in the early 1990s, even Amstrad have been hit by stiff competition in the home and business personal computer market, reporting pre-tax losses of some £71 million in the year to 30 June 1992. This is the first time in the history of the company that its results have shown a pre-tax loss, with profits still at some £20 million the previous year.

Sinclair's rationale behind the sale of the one arm of his business which had been proved a success was that it enabled him to continue as an innovator and developer of new products. While his short-term business strategy – to perceive new consumer requirements and satisfy them with exciting new products – proved largely successful, there appears to have been no medium- or long-term strategy to build up a stable business based on the gradual evolution of these new products. He described his role as one of 'initiating markets', but as these markets matured and consumer requirements became more demanding, Sinclair Research was unable to respond.

Sinclair is a fine example of an individual who is an expert in his own field, who has discovered – or indeed created – a market demand for his product, and yet who does not succeed in business terms. Although attempts were made in 1985 to avoid the collapse of his computer business, by making payment deals with suppliers and cutting his workforce, it seems that market confidence in his business and, more importantly, in Sinclair himself had declined too far ever to recover fully.

Failure of this type does not necessarily occur on such a dramatic or public scale. A problem which many small and new businesses face is that of building up stability rather than impressing the market place with spectacular new products. There is clearly a temptation, especially in high technology sectors, to keep ahead of the competition by constantly developing and upgrading technology rather than concentrating on a proven product. There is an increasing awareness in the business computer hardware market, for example, that it is not always necessary to use state-of-the-art technology.

# Type 2 turnaround

ACORN COMPUTER GROUP PLC

A similar fate could have befallen the Acorn Computer Group Plc, had a drastic turnaround plan not been implemented. Like Sinclair, Acorn placed a strong emphasis on research and development, although the latter company was far more successful in attaining high standards of reliability and quality. In less than five years, Acorn had become a City favourite, and was capitalized on the Unlisted Securities Market at some £200 million.

The BBC micro-computer, widely used in schools, had proved an enormous success and Acorn were attempting to break into similar markets in Germany and the USA, apparently a sensible marketing strategy, as opposed to trying to compete in additional sectors of the UK market.

Problems began to emerge, however. The German and US markets proved more difficult to compete in than had been anticipated, and demand was also beginning to drop off in the UK. Coupled with this, the development of a junior version of the BBC micro-computer had been delayed with the result that it was not available for the hoped-for sales boom at Christmas 1983. By the time it appeared on the market, the market for home computers was already satisfied by cheaper products.

In financial terms, the problem which was becoming most pressing was cashflow. As was the case with Sinclair Research, Christmas sales in 1984 had again not reached expectations, and stocks had piled up. At the same time, orders had already been placed with the subcontractors who manufactured the computers for Acorn. Cash inflows were adequate only to pay the company's overheads, but not its subcontractors.

Had decisions not been taken quickly, receivership would probably have been the next step. However, the management team decided there were two possible courses of action. The first was to sell the company, which they were reluctant to do. The second was to make an attempt at refinancing.

The refinancing option was accepted, and involved formal

arrangements with major creditors for the re-scheduling of debts, a cutback of overheads, including staff redundancies and the closure of major projects, revised loan arrangements with the company's bankers and investment by an external equity investor.

In March 1985, with the above aims achieved within a matter of weeks, the emphasis within the business was on sustaining – if not increasing – their level of sales, and in collecting cash. A great deal of energy and planning was put into the process. However, a factor which the management team could not have forecast was a downturn in sales during April and May 1985, which was not confined to Acorn but affected the entire micro-computer market.

A second reconstruction was devised, which required a further substantial investment by the external equity holder, Olivetti, and an agreement with major creditors to write off half of the outstanding debt due to them from Acorn, the other half being paid in cash on the date of the reconstruction. Creditors and Acorn's bankers agreed to the proposals, and, in August 1985, their shares were trading once again on the Unlisted Securities Market, after two periods of suspension.

Perhaps the essential difference between Sinclair and Acorn is the desire to rescue the business and to return it to profitable trading. While Sinclair was concerned primarily with the innovative aspects of his business rather than building a stable and successful trading entity, the management team at Acorn displayed the opposite reaction. Although this meant that eventually Acorn had to relinquish 21 per cent of the equity of the company, this form of refinancing was considered preferable to selling the entire company – again, the opposite reaction to that of Sinclair.

A major difference between the two businesses was that Acorn's products were considered reliable and of good quality, and the company had established itself safely in the UK educational market, in conjunction with assistance from both the BBC and the government. Sinclair had not created such a solid niche in the market: it was the cheapness of his computer products which had initially attracted the consumer.

# Type 3 failure: 'Slow death'

Type 3 failures vary again, in that they have often traded successfully for a number of years, and may seem to have achieved a high degree of stability, and have built up a respectable reputation. Decline begins when a combination of problems, such as a failed project or overtrading, occur, and the business finds that sales and profits have fallen, or it requires a large loan and then has difficulty in meeting the repayments. Although the financial health of the business may have declined considerably, it may then level out. However, it may take only one more blow now for the business to fail completely. Under normal circumstances, a business may happily survive and trade through the hazards described above. It is generally when they occur in combination that the business's survival is called into question.

## ROLLS-ROYCE

Rolls-Royce, the aerospace parent company of the group, provides an illustration of a Type 3 collapse. Although the company continues to trade it had to be rescued by the government in 1971, after huge debts had built up resulting from its aero-engine contract with Lockheed. Rolls-Royce had established its name over decades, diversifying during the First World War from its activities as a prestige motor car manufacturer to the aero-engine field. That a business which appeared so stable could fail came as a shock both inside and outside the company.

The report produced for the Minister for Trade and Industry on Rolls-Royce's failure blamed its decline into receivership, among other factors, on a lack of attention to the financial position of the company by those in ultimate control, and a number of technical engineering problems, although this conclusion was not agreed by all experts. It does seem that these factors were present, and they were undoubtedly associated with the RB211 contract which Rolls-Royce were attempting to secure with Lockheed, which would allow the company a major breakthrough in the North American market.

The RB211 contract, in terms of marketing strategy, was clearly a positive move on the part of Rolls-Royce, but the overriding attitudes towards the financial management of the project were disastrous. A lack of cost control in the past had left Rolls-Royce ill-prepared for a project which demanded detailed appraisal of the investment in research needed to develop the RB211 engine to the required specification. The resources available were already limited by the financial drain placed on Rolls-Royce several years earlier when it had purchased its competitor, Bristol Siddely.

Rolls-Royce were successful in securing the contract, but further problems were to follow when Lockheed specified a requirement for a more powerful engine than the RB211-06 which had been developed. This clearly called for further investment in developing new technology, but it seemed to be assumed that the technology would evolve as the project progressed. It did not. The problems resulting from a fixed-price contract for which the costing had not been evaluated properly were evident.

In fact, the information required for costing appraisal, budgetary control and financial forecasting appears to have been available. However, it was not absorbed or acted upon by a board which was dominated by its Chairman and Chief Executive, Sir Denning Pearson, and where engineering issues seem to have taken precedence over financial ones.

The RB211-22 was produced to the required specification after a modification to its design at the last minute – but not soon enough to meet the delivery dates specified by Lockheed, for which a financial penalty was suffered.

Rolls-Royce attempted to solve its immediate financial problems by requesting further bank support, which was granted on condition that a new Chairman and Chief Executive were appointed. The change in management was not effective, and in 1971 the receiver was called in and parts of the Rolls-Royce group were sold to the government. In fact, with further investment by the government the RB211 project became a success, and did allow Rolls-Royce to establish itself as a market contender in North America. However, this required dramatic changes by Sir Kenneth Keith, Rolls-Royce's new Chairman in 1972. Proper systems of communicating, accounting and costing information were introduced, together with a clearly defined management structure which ensured that productivity levels could be assessed and improved to give the company a chance of survival.

Rolls-Royce was hit again in the early 1980s by a drastic fall in demand in the United States, and made a serious gamble in deciding to invest in new plant, in research and in rethinking its production processes with the aim of reducing manufacturing costs and improving the company's competitive position. Unlike the early stages of the RB211 contract, this was a calculated gamble which paid off, and left the company in a far healthier state than it had been ten years previously.

It could be said that Rolls-Royce's failure stemmed from a lack of financial and management communication. Although the company was well established, had built a reputation for quality and in that sense could be considered a success, its systems of financial communication had not developed on the same scale. During the war, government contracts for aero-engines had been based on a formula which included a profit for the manufacturer, providing no incentive for tight cost control, and proper costing systems had not subsequently been developed. When faced with a contract such as Lockheed, the board was simply not prepared for the more competitive conditions under which the RB211 engine needed to be developed.

## Type 3 turnaround

### VICKERS PLC

Vickers plc, the engineering company, had on the other hand suffered problems which were not entirely of its own making, in that parts of the company were nationalized then sold back. Its medium- and long-term strategies had lost coherence, and the final blow came when in 1977 the government nationalized the shipbuilding and aircraft businesses which Vickers had built up.

The merger in 1980 with Rolls-Royce Motors, which had been floated off after the collapse of its parent company in 1971, was greeted by many external observers as a largely negative move which was likely to result in failure. However, it was regarded by the management teams within the two merging businesses as a logical means to strengthen both companies. The Chairman and Chief Executive of Vickers recognized that if the newly merged companies were to be successful then improved management structures and communication were essential to ensure that staff understood the drastic changes that needed to be implemented. Without these improvements there would be little hope of success.

A coherent strategy was formulated, with a clear policy of building up those parts of the company which could operate as significant competitors in growing markets, both in the UK and internationally. A period of fairly ruthless but carefully planned divestment of those businesses which did not satisfy these criteria and acquisition of other businesses to strengthen the company followed.

Financial reporting and planning were also a critical part of the overall strategy. Systems were implemented such that management reports on prior month results were available within two weeks of the month end, so that problems, in particular those of cashflow, could be identified at the earliest possible opportunity, and results could be compared with those projected in budgets. The forward planning process also underwent changes, with the implementation of an annual three-stage planning process incorporating strategic plans, an overall business plan and detailed operating budgets.

Management structure and the quality of management teams were equally important in ensuring that changes in the company were instituted as effectively and smoothly as possible. Communication with staff at all levels was a high priority, and commitment at management levels was enhanced by incentive schemes for senior management based on return on capital employed.

Although all of these changes were positive, it is financial results which ultimately make or break a company. In this respect as well, Vickers succeeded, with earnings per share increasing from 14p in 1982 to 40.7p in 1986. The company was equally proud of its vastly improved profit per employee ratio, which showed an even more dramatic increase from some £750 in 1982 to around £3,400 in 1986.

Many of the changes undertaken within the new Vickers group of companies were brave ones, needing a high degree of clear-sightedness about its strengths and weaknesses. The divestment of companies which were judged to be unable to contribute to the new strategy of future growth of market share and profitability involved staff redundancies, and in some respects the new policy could not be a welcome one.

Internal reporting systems also underwent radical changes in order that the trading progress of all businesses within the new company could be monitored tightly at all levels. At the risk of drawing over-simplified conclusions, this appears to be one of the major differences between the failed Rolls-Royce aerospace project and the new Vickers plc.

In spite of its improved financial performance in the 1980s, Vickers has not been immune to the recessionary pressures of the early 1990s. Rolls-Royce Motors' luxury car sales have been hit throughout 1992, with resulting job losses of some 950 employees: the workforce has thus been cut by around 57 per cent in two years, in addition to the redundancies of the 1980s.

Data Magnetics, Sinclair and Rolls-Royce present three contrasting cases of failure. Acorn and Vickers, on the other hand, illustrate how a change in management and strategy can help a company to survive.

## Problems of failing businesses

The types of problem observed in each of the three failure trajectories may well share common factors. However, it would not be accurate to categorize these issues as particular to certain types of business: most businesses fail from a combination of adverse factors. Analysts have produced numerous lists of these factors, and it is difficult to compile a definitive list, but those which arise frequently are discussed below. Specific managerial issues are not included here, but are examined in chapter 3.

Some of the most significant issues which contribute to the decline and failure of a business are:

- high gearing
- overtrading
- inadequate sales
- reliance on a big project
- competitive weakness
- lack of vision
- over-diversification / lack of synergy.

## High gearing

High gearing means that a high proportion of a business's capital employed is in the form of loans rather than equity. There are a number of measurements of gearing, some of which include both long- and various forms of short-term debt, and some of which include only long-term debt. However, the essential difference between a business financed by loans and one financed by equity is that the former carries (usually) fixed interest payments and the latter pays out dividends.

An appropriate level of gearing (i.e. the proportion of a business's capital employed which is represented by debt) does, of course, vary from business to business and between industries. However, a high level of gearing can leave a business in an extremely vulnerable position, particularly if economic recession occurs. If profit margins drop as a result of a downturn in demand, and at the same time interest rates rise, a small business can be quickly and seriously affected by interest payments which it can no longer sustain with reasonable ease. In short, a company which has high gearing should be regarded with caution particularly when economic conditions are poor, and this factor emerges as a relatively common cause of failure.

## Overtrading

If properly planned, expansion should not lead to overtrading and cause collapse. Problems tend to arise with business expansion when the specific motive behind the expansion is to increase turnover and market share – to become a more significant player in a given market. The danger when attempting to achieve this goal is that profit margins are sacrificed – either knowingly or unconsciously – in order to stimulate sales.

A further danger is that cashflow requirements are likely to increase to finance higher levels of stocks and debtors, for example. Furthermore, if profit margins decrease, then the ratio of interest payments to profits increases, and the business may well find that although business may appear to be improving in terms of turnover, it is in fact less able to support the interest payments on its loan or overdraft facilities.

It is easy to fall prey to the risks of overtrading unintentionally, and to find that serious problems of cashflow arise when it might be assumed that business performance should be improving. It is dangerous to emphasize turnover as a yardstick against which to measure overall business performance. Planned or actual growth in turnover should always be considered and calculated in conjunction with the associated costs and the effects on profit margins and cashflow.

## Inadequate sales

In contrast to overtrading, inadequate sales appears a more obvious factor which might lead to business failure. In an established business, this may occur because of a decline in demand due to economic conditions and is likely to be extremely difficult to remedy, particularly when the exercise of analysing and reducing costs wherever possible has already been carried out. For a new business, however, the reasons may be quite different. If no budgeting was carried out to calculate the level of sales required to achieve breakeven point, then the business may quickly find it is simply unable to support its overheads. Methods of setting a price are outlined in chapters 4 and 5.

However, even if realistic selling prices have been calculated and breakeven analysis carried out, this is no guarantee that the product or service will achieve the target level of turnover. This might occur for various reasons, including straightforward factors such as poor quality or unreliable service, which mean that repeat sales are not made, or poor market research, so that it is discovered too late that there are too many competitors in the area, or that the product has become outdated.

## Big project

The effects of inadequate sales are similar to those experienced when too much reliance is placed on a big project. A big project can be not only the development of a major new product or service which requires excessive resources, but also an ambitious acquisition programme, a major piece of research, reliance on a very small number of substantial customers or indeed any project undertaken by the company which is significant in terms of the available resources within the company.

However, it should be remembered that it is not necessarily the project itself which can cause a business to fail, but the way it is managed. If it is properly planned and budgeted then it is likely that the problems which will inevitably arise can be solved, be they financial or not. If, for example, a product development programme is monitored regularly, and proves to be costing more than was forecast whilst not producing the desired results, then decisions can be taken whether or not to continue the project by reference to the forecast costs and objectives. If no such planning has been carried out, there is a far greater likelihood that both time and financial resources will be poured into the project long after it should have been discontinued – simply because there was no yardstick against which to measure it.

The Rolls-Royce RB211 contract is a good example of a big project which (arguably) resulted in disaster. A history of poor budgeting within the company meant that the development of the engine cost far more than had been expected – without producing the desired result. In this case, it was not a simple question of being able to discontinue the research. However, better communication of accounting and technical information might have warned Rolls-Royce at an earlier stage that serious problems, both financial and technical, existed.

## Competitive weakness

Competitive weakness as a cause of failure usually results from one of various underlying factors. A business may suffer from newly available cheap imports, for example, or may be a victim of technological change, a particular problem for businesses operating in markets where technology is constantly upgraded, such as computer hardware. A business which is familiar with its markets and keeps informed of changing requirements and new developments is obviously less likely to be caught out in this way, but for small businesses this can still present problems if, say, it has invested heavily in a product or equipment which is unexpectedly superseded. Such a business could, of course, also fall into big project category.

Competitive weakness can also result from losing touch with a market. This need not be the outcome of major changes in that market, technological or otherwise, but a failure to take notice of improvements to products or services introduced by competitors, for example. This is a factor which a business can control, or at least be aware of.

A problem faced by many small businesses is that of finding themselves to be a very small player in a large market. Whilst the dangers of over-specialization are clear, the risks of trying to break into a large and already competitive market are equally great. If a business is unable to create some form of niche in a large market, its chances of success will be reduced.

Also stemming from a knowledge of its market sector is a business's reaction to competition, whether from a new competitor or from a sales drive initiated by an existing competitor. For a business operating in a highly specialized market sector, it will be easier to keep abreast of developments made by competitors. In markets where a large number of competitors are operating, it may prove possible to monitor only local competition, say. In either case, if little or no regard is paid to developments made by competing businesses in the belief that customers will remain loyal, a business will be particularly unable to respond if customer loyalty proves to have been overestimated. This problem can be especially difficult to deal with in high-technology markets, where a small company may simply not have the resources to respond quickly to technical advances in its field. For these businesses, their planning and overall strategy needs to be even more carefully formulated and reviewed regularly.

However, the problem is not confined to markets which are subject to rapid change. The proprietor of a prosperous news-agent and general store in a small town became concerned when he discovered that a rival shop selling much the same range of goods was opening very nearby. It was unlikely that the town would be able to support two such similar shops, and further-more, the proprietor was unable to see how the town would benefit significantly from the competition.

For him the immediate problem was how to retain his customers without cutting prices to such a degree that the business would no longer be profitable. The alternative was to diversify into a completely different range of goods which was not available elsewhere in the town – but this also represented a major risk, since he could not be sure of levels of demand.

He eventually decided that the most sensible course of action in the short term was to monitor the performance of his own business extremely closely so that the effects of the competition could be quantified accurately. This would not solve the prob-lem, nor relieve his concern that he might go out of business. It was simply the most constructive path open to him. In fact, a year later, turnover had decreased by around 20 per cent, which was far less than he had feared and meant that the business was still viable. However, it could just as easily have been his business which suffered, and not his competitor's.

## Lack of vision

Lack of vision in a business can manifest itself in various forms, from misreading market requirements to inadequate marketing of a product or service.

A basic error is that of proceeding with a business concept after it has become clear that it will not succeed. How much time is required to prove the viability of a concept will be different for every business, and the most significant factor dictating this timescale is likely to be the availability of financial resources. If these are severely limited, then the failure of a bad idea will probably occur quickly, say, within two years. If financial limitations are less stringent – perhaps personal finance is available to support the business for a longer period – then there will be a temptation to continue the business in the hope that success is just around the corner. Succumbing to such a temptation in these circumstances where it is clear (at least to an external observer) that the business concept is not going to succeed can lead to personal ruin as well as the failure of the business.

A failure of vision might also be demonstrated in businesses where it is clear that a complete rethink of the running of the business is required, but management content themselves with tinkering.

The important point here is to have a clear idea of what goals the business is trying to meet, and to draw up detailed plans formulating the action required to achieve those goals. Having determined the required action and established whether or not it is feasible – whether adequate finance is available, for example – it is important either to see the plans through, to revise them, or to drop them altogether. Being content with making minor changes which only partially match up to business plans, so that no tangible positive goal is achieved will benefit nobody. It is likely that the only result will be a loss of time and potentially money.

Similar problems can arise where the driving force behind the business is a specialist, and indeed an expert, within their own field but either lacks or is not interested in the skills required to transform their expertise into a viable business concept. The most common example of the latter case is the inventor who is almost entirely concerned with the development of a product without much regard for its marketability. The lifespan of a business suffering from this problem is almost necessarily a short one, since financial support is likely to be withdrawn at an early stage. The former case arises more frequently, and often because an individual is simply inexperienced in running a business. With effective support from bankers, accountants and other professionals, there is still no reason why the business should not succeed. The problem here is the recognition of this factor as a problem at an early enough stage.

## Over-diversification / lack of synergy

Problems of a different nature can arise where a business tries to over-diversify, and is unable to devote sufficient attention to the efficient running of various arms of a business which have grown up without proper planning. A business might, quite sensibly, perceive a market need for a product or service which is complementary to their existing business activity. For example, a small business which has built up a good reputation selling specialized second-hand industrial machinery might see a need to provide machine servicing and repairs. This would be a logical extension to the business, given that a customer base would already exist, and appropriate contacts would already have been made. However, a less sensible move would be a decision to diversify into the sale of a different type of machinery, in which it lacked technical expertise or knowledge of the market. The aim in diversification should be to build on existing skills, knowledge and resources, rather than to take the risk of moving into new markets where the business has no track record or expertise.

This might appear obvious, but errors are often made by businesses which believe they see a lucrative opportunity which is unrelated to their existing activities. The term 'synergy' is often used in connection with business diversification or acquisitions, referring essentially to the goal of making the sum of the whole greater than the sum of the parts of the business (i.e. $2 + 2 = 5$). A lack of synergy, or cohesion between the individual elements of a business, can quickly lead to a lack of focus and confusion as to its longer-term aims.

## External factors

The factors described above fall largely within the control of the management of a business. There are, of course, broader economic issues which will affect a business and over which it will be able to exert less control. These are discussed in more detail in chapter 7, but it is worth mentioning in passing that these can contribute significantly to the failure of a business if it is unable to respond to them.

Economic recession is perhaps the biggest nightmare for small businesses, and one which has resulted directly or indirectly in ever-increasing numbers of business failures throughout the past five years. Businesses which already have high levels of bank borrowings become particularly vulnerable as interest costs rise in proportion to profits, and lenders become increasingly concerned for the safety of their loans. When inflation has been high and levels of demand are less secure, the effects of setbacks which might not have represented too great a problem in a more healthy economic climate can take on more dramatic proportions.

It has been said that the healthy business should be able to continue to trade throughout periods of recession, and that it is those businesses which were already in poor financial shape which fail. This may hold true for the early stages of a recession. However, when consumer and business confidence does not improve, it is inevitable that previously healthy businesses also become vulnerable. This vulnerability may continue for some time after the end of a recession, when business owners and managers might assume that improved economic conditions will have fairly swift results for their business. This might hold true for some, but there will be many struggling to regain their stability for some time.

### Disaster and bad luck

Both disaster and bad luck are rarely observed as causes of failure. Of course, a whole chain of adverse events might combine to bring about the failure of a company, but in reality this is extremely rare. A single disaster or piece of bad luck – such as the loss of a major customer, the breakdown of a vital piece of manufacturing equipment or the refusal of a bank manager to extend an additional overdraft facility – should not bring about the failure of a business which is essentially healthy. It may well be a serious setback which requires the redrafting of plans for the immediate future, but in normal conditions businesses can recover from such setbacks.

In times of adverse economic conditions, when businesses are already suffering from, for example, high interest rates and poor levels of consumer demand, the disasters mentioned above can indeed be the factors which push a business over the brink into failure. However, these businesses are generally the ones which have already suffered, and whose results and financial stability have already deteriorated.

It will never be possible to define all the problems which will lead a business into decline, or to prescribe failsafe cures for those problems. However, the issues and examples described above should provide business owners and managers with some thoughts for the dangers which many businesses face at some point. It is worth reiterating that the most important – and probably the most difficult – step is to recognize and acknowledge these problems if they arise.

# 3. **Managerial style**

There is little doubt that bad management is the factor most frequently cited for business failure or poor performance. It could hardly be otherwise, since the most remarkable product or service alone does not create a successful business. Conversely, the most effective managers will not necessarily create a stable and profitable business from a poor product or service. During periods of economic recession, it may be argued that there is less that managers can do to avoid failure or declining performance. However, it is probably true to say that good managers are less likely to fall prey to the pitfalls which can undermine business performance.

Much has been written on the subject of business management and managerial style, although less which concentrates on the aspects of management which commonly contribute to business failure. In a small business, where the management team may consist of one or two individuals, much of what is written for larger companies may seem largely irrelevant. However, the basic principles will not differ.

While it is not possible to define exactly the type of management faults or defects which may contribute to business failure, there are certain factors which are often observed in failing businesses, including:

- the autocrat;
- the weak business owner / manager;
- the weak finance function;
- lack of response to constraints or change;
- lack of defined management role and responsibility;
- poor communication, either internal or external.

Some of these factors were included by John Argenti in his 'A-score' analysis, which he devised as a tool for predicting business failure, and which is described in chapter 6.

## The autocrat

An autocratic management style need not manifest itself in aggressive qualities, although this is often the case. It may also be demonstrated in a managing director, senior partner or proprietor who appears to listen to the suggestions and ideas of colleagues, but who quietly disregards them when reaching decisions. However, more common is the individual who imposes decisions with little or no consultation, and is secretive towards colleagues and employees about, for example, business performance and plans for the future. These characteristics tend to be most common where the individual wants to retain absolute control over the business. While this may arise out of necessity in a very small and young business which is essentially run and managed by one person, it is rarely the most productive management style as the business begins to grow.

> This became evident in a small family-owned manufacturing company. After twenty years of reasonably successful trading, the company had grown to employ twenty-five production staff, and was apparently managed by the managing director, his wife (also a director and shareholder) and one other recently appointed director who was keen to take an active management role in the company. In reality, all decisions were taken by the managing director, with little attention paid to the suggestions and views of others, either within or outside the company. This policy may have been adequate while the company was in its infancy, but ceased to yield positive results as the company grew. In fact, his desire for absolute control was such that a newly appointed external accountant who discussed the company's financial position and potential for improvement with the new director quickly found himself replaced for an alleged breach of confidence. The autocrat was unable to accept that the business had grown to a size where more effective management could be achieved by the combined skills and abilities of the directors as a team than by himself alone.
>
> With more accurate systems of cost control over manufacturing processes and of determining selling prices, which were

based very much upon rough estimates, the company could have improved its gross profit margins with relative ease. However, the managing director was not in favour of implementing any new systems of monitoring and control which did not originate from him and which would require 'revealing' financial information to individuals other than himself. He simply could not take the more objective view that this would play a very positive role in benefiting the company – and himself. The company continues to trade, but only after reducing its staff (a decision taken by the managing director) in an attempt to cut costs.

How to take action to change the attitude of an autocrat is an extremely tricky question. Almost by definition, even the most constructive suggestions concerning the management of the business from fellow managers, partners or employees will probably be disregarded. It might be tempting simply to try to take action or decisions without the autocrat's knowledge, but this approach does not address the root of the problem. A more effective approach is likely to be one which uses individual issues or problems in the business to illustrate that the discussion and pooling of ideas can bring greater benefit both to the business and the individual.

An associated problem in smaller businesses is the delegation of responsibility. This can prove difficult for even the most fair-minded of business owners and managers who have previously been accustomed to taking all responsibility for the management of the business. As the business grows and additional managers or partners are needed, the re-allocation of responsibilities in itself may be a straightforward exercise. The acceptance that additional management skills are required in the business is probably the greatest hurdle for the owner to cross.

However, the acceptance that others are equally capable, once involved in the business, of taking decisions or initiating action can take some time. There is always a danger of losing the additional time gained through excessive checking and looking over the shoulder of new managers. While a certain level of guidance and consultation will be needed in the early stages, business owners should ensure that they do not develop auto-cratic tendencies, but rather use the additional time available to them as constructively as possible to develop the business.

An autocratic style of management should not, however, be confused with a one-man band, which is essentially owned, managed and operated by a single individual. There is a vast difference between a person who builds up a small business more or less single-handed and an autocrat who rules a slightly larger concern without discussion or consultation with affected parties who should be able to make a valuable contribution to decision-making.

The significance of the autocrat in business decline or failure is probably clear: there is an increasing danger as the business develops and grows that the management skills of the autocrat are no longer adequate to cope with the decisions and problems which will inevitably arise.

## The weak or inexperienced business owner / manager

Like the autocrat, a weak or inexperienced owner or manager is also likely to run into problems which result from defective decision-making, but for different reasons. Decisions may be made on the basis of faulty information or understanding, which the manager is simply not skilled enough to recognize. Alternatively, advice will be sought from various sources – such as professional advisers, business associates, literature and the media – but will not be put to best use or will only be partially acted upon, again through a lack of proper understanding of the implications and consequences for the business.

It should also be pointed out that managers of considerable experience within large organizations who subsequently start up or become involved in a small business can easily fall into this trap. Coping with the problems of, say, a senior sales executive responsible for a substantial sales team does not necessarily provide the experience relevant to running a smaller business.

This is illustrated by a limited company set up by two

individuals. One supplied the finance to provide it with working capital and the other was to be responsible for the day-to-day running of the business, a smart, 'open all hours' type shop, selling groceries, tobacco and newspapers and magazines. The director with responsibility for running the business was a successful and experienced sales manager, who had taken voluntary redundancy from a large retail store. Although sophisticated tills and computer equipment were purchased, no advice was taken as to how these would be best used to exercise control and monitor performance. Although prices were a little above average, business was brisk and there was a general feeling that the shop's financial performance was encouraging.

However, the bank overdraft continued to increase when it was felt that no overdraft should be required, and eventually an accountant was asked to look at business performance, with the specific aim of identifying the stock lines which were least profitable. It was discovered that many selling prices had been miscalculated, so that margins were far smaller than had been intended, and that there had been pilfering on a large scale. Although stock control systems had been discussed, no system had actually been implemented, and stocks were purchased on a wholly *ad hoc* basis, depending on what was running low. No single individual had responsibility for ordering stock, and given the high turnover of part-time employees, it was not surprising that no coherent system of monitoring or control had been followed.

By the time accounts had been prepared, the position had worsened still further, and the directors were horrified at the level of liabilities which had been allowed to build up. As well as the bank overdraft, substantial amounts were owed to suppliers, who were becoming increasingly restive at not receiving payments when they fell due. A decision was taken to close the shop and to liquidate the company: the director who had provided the finance was simply not prepared to invest any further, and no means of improving the business's financial position within a reasonably short time span could be devised.

At this stage, an extremely serious development occurred. It emerged that the director who had been responsible for the management of the business had given personal guarantees to several suppliers as security for their credit facilities. On discovering they would not receive full payment of the amounts owing to them by the company, these suppliers demanded payment of their outstanding invoices from the director himself. The end result of this action was that the director was unable to satisfy the payments and was declared personally bankrupt. Besides considerable distress to him and his family, his subsequent business activities have been severely curtailed by the bankruptcy action. Discussions later revealed that he was completely unaware of the implications and risks of giving personal guarantees to creditors.

This was a business venture which was fraught with problems from the beginning. Although both directors had gained considerable experience within large organizations, they discovered quickly that this did not equip them with the particular expertise required to run a small business effectively. Adequate consultation and thought as to how the business could be controlled *before* trading commenced was clearly missing. Perhaps the most important lesson learnt was the danger of signing any form of agreement without fully understanding its implications. This may be an extreme case, but it is not an isolated one, and the distress it caused should not be underestimated: this director considers himself fortunate not to have been forced into the sale of the family home to satisfy the business's debts.

Weakness or inexperience in the management of a small business does not have to be a reason either for not setting up a business or for its failure. However, if business owners or managers under these circumstances ignore the extent of the responsibilities and dangers which face them, they could easily fall into the same trap. Careful and detailed planning and appropriate consultation with advisers – both individuals such as accountants and solicitors, and bodies such as Enterprise Agencies – will help to draw attention to the areas of business management in which the business owner or manager lacks expertise.

# The weak finance function

Argenti's analysis specifically refers to a weak Finance Director as a significant factor in business failure. In the scenario he describes, this is often a situation encouraged by an autocrat, in order to maintain the maximum degree of control over the management of a company.

In a small business, the circumstances may well be different, in that the owner or manager who is responsible for controlling the business may also be responsible for the finance function. However, the principle remains the same. However good the accounting systems and the quality of information generated (and remember that 'good' does not have to mean 'sophisticated'), they are of no use to the business unless they are acted upon and used as one of the factors in decision-making.

Clearly, there will be certain issues which the owner or manager cannot ignore – a bank overdraft which is slowly but steadily increasing, a growing number of requests from suppliers for payment of their invoices, obvious cash constraints which curtail plans to develop the business and so on. However, there may be considerably less awareness of the finance function as a whole in the business beyond an administrative need for records to be maintained for, say, VAT purposes or to comply with Companies Act regulations.

A small printing business whose main source of work was the printing of stationery and leaflets for local businesses maintained simple but accurate manual accounting records – a cash book, sales day book, purchase day book and petty cash book. These were written up regularly and all documents were carefully and logically filed. However, the wealth of information they provided was not used constructively: bookkeeping, although meticulously carried out, was not seen as an integral part of the management of the business. For example, although the proprietor kept a watchful eye on the bank balance as shown by bank statements, no thought was given to the active management of cash inflows from customers or outflows in the form of payments to suppliers. The necessity for a small but expensive bank overdraft could probably have been avoided if customers had been chased for payment of sales invoices as they fell due, and by changing the policy of paying all suppliers' invoices, regardless of their due dates, at the end of the month in which they were received.

A new and more astute book-keeper made these suggestions, amongst others, when reviewing the business's records and financial position. They were welcomed by the proprietor, who was then spurred into looking at other aspects of the financial management of the business for further straightforward means of improving, primarily, the business's cash-flow.

This is a very simple example, but serves to illustrate the point that the finance and book-keeping functions in a small business should not be regarded as separate and purely administrative exercises. Financial management *is* an important factor within any business, and should never be overlooked when decisions for the future of the business are being worked out.

A second case concerns a small electrical service and repair business which appeared to have avoided this trap. An external management accountant maintained the business's records on computer, and produced monthly management accounts, including detailed debtors, creditors and stock listings. All of these, with the exception of the stock listing, were used regularly and the overall level of financial management in the business appeared good.

However, it was later discovered when a physical stock count was carried out that the stock listing – which contained details of several hundred different items of both high and low value – bore little relation to the actual level of stocks held by the business. It was clearly not practical, with a large number of very low value items, to carry out frequent physical stock checks, but this could easily have been achieved for the relatively low number of high value lines.

It should be borne in mind that the value of stocks has a direct impact on the calculation of the business's cost of sales (in this case, cost of sales was represented by the cost of stocks sold and used in repairs plus the cost of direct labour).

Cost of stocks used    =    Opening stock value
           Add:    Purchases
           Less:    Closing stock value

It follows that if the level of closing stock is materially wrong, the business's profitability will be distorted, since

Gross profit =       Sales
         Less:   Cost of sales

In this case, it was discovered at the business's year-end stock count that the value of stocks according to the stock listing differed significantly from the actual stock held. Because the differences had built up over a long period, it was extremely difficult to find reasons for the discrepancies. However, the monetary effect on the business's year-end accounts (compared with the management accounts) was large enough to reduce the gross profit to a degree that it only just covered the business's overheads.

It was immediately decided that physical stock checks would be carried out on all high-value items on a monthly basis, to prevent the problem arising in subsequent periods: this would take no longer than an hour every month. Given the efforts which had been made to monitor and control other aspects of the business's financial performance, it was felt that this would be time well spent.

A weak finance function therefore does not simply mean the lack of a finance specialist or poor accounting records, although these factors can of course be significant. The more important point is that the financial information needs of the business have to be recognized, and this information incorporated into the overall management of the business, not regarded as a separate function.

While a weak finance function alone will not in itself cause the decline or failure of a business, a lack of financial management information can obviously have a significant effect on informed decision-making. Taking the wrong decision *can* affect future business survival. In a smaller business, the introduction of adequate systems to record and monitor financial information must ultimately be the responsibility of the business owner or manager.

## Lack of response to change / constraints

Although this issue is also covered elsewhere in the text, it is worth expanding further because of its significance in the development of a business. A lack of response to any business factor which clearly demands action – or at least considered thought – tends to be symptomatic of a head-in-the-sand approach to management. Plenty of guidance on how to be a pro-active manager (one who initiates action rather than reacting to events) can be found in texts dealing specifically with the problems of management, but these tend to be directed more at individuals working within larger organizations.

In a small business, it can be difficult enough dealing with problematic issues on a day-to-day basis, without also looking ahead to assess how, for example, economic, social or technological changes in the future could affect the business. However, it is as well to be aware of any particular factors which could have a significant adverse effect on the business, and this will largely be a matter of common sense: technological issues will be of significance in a computer hardware business so far as their sales are concerned, but probably not in a catering business.

Economic changes can have a major impact on sales and, for example, businesses which sell goods or services which are regarded as non-essential may be amongst the first to suffer a drop in sales in times of economic recession. Such goods or services might include luxury household goods, new motor vehicles, corporate entertainment and hospitality, some types of staff training and so on.

While changes of any sort will have a detrimental effect on some businesses, there will be other businesses which can benefit by fulfilling a need in their market which did not previously exist, or whose form has changed.

For example, as consumers become more aware of environmental issues, there has been an increasing market for products which are more environmentally friendly, in the broadest sense of the word. Accordingly, paper products which contain re-cycled paper, cosmetics which have not been tested on animals and aerosols which do not contain CFCs have enjoyed growing popularity. There are also products such as fridges whose manufacture is now subject to regulation as a result of increased concern for the environment. Of course, such issues will affect a relatively small proportion of businesses in terms of the image and presentation of their goods to consumers, but for these businesses, this factor could be a significant one.

Other changes, such as the introduction of more stringent health and safety regulations, can have far-reaching effects for a small business.

> A countryside pub, which relied on its food sales for a significant proportion of its income, became a victim when an inspection revealed that its kitchens did not measure up to the required standards in many respects, a fact the chef had warned of well in advance of the revised regulations. The expenditure needed to replace its fittings and equipment was far in excess of what the business could afford within the imposed deadline.
>
> The outcome was that the pub was no longer able to serve food, and lost both regular and passing custom as a result. In addition, two of the staff lost their jobs as a direct result. The chef was particularly bitter that he had warned of the problem and advised on the gradual replacement of fittings and equipment, so that the business could spread the expenditure over a longer period of time.

Technological developments are similarly affecting a growing range of products. The specific factors which dictate whether a product quickly becomes outmoded or overtaken by a rival are various, and examples are numerous. Betamax and VHS videos were in direct competition at the time of their launch, and although Betamax were perceived by some to be a better product technically, it was VHS which won the battle to secure consumer loyalty. Whether this was a result of pricing, marketing, perceived quality or durability or some other factor is not entirely clear, but Betamax were quickly forced out of the market. It is not fair to accuse the manufacturer of lack of response to this change or to the constraints which were necessarily imposed, but the case does illustrate the speed with which markets can change or loyalties shift.

A different problem again has affected the development of laser vision technology. Similar to compact disks in format, laser vision disks provide not only sound but images which are transmitted on a television screen, fulfilling much the same function as a VCR. In spite of several launches, the product does not appear to have found a secure foothold in the home entertainment market, which seems to have remained largely loyal to VCRs. It could be argued that there is a similarity with the competition with the well-established vinyl record market and that for CDs, in that new equipment is required by the consumer in order to play the disks. However, CDs now have an established market in spite of their relatively high individual cost, whereas laser vision technology has not.

In high-technology markets, and particularly when two or more directly competing products are launched at about the same time, it can be almost impossible to predict which will succeed and which will fail, and equally difficult to discern the reasons. However thorough the market research, and however careful the marketing and advertising campaigns and pricing policy, these markets can be fickle, and there must be many products which logically should have succeeded but which have not.

The same principles and problems apply to the (perhaps) smaller businesses which manufacture parts for these products. A small component may represent a significant proportion of projected turnover for a small business. While there can be no guaranteed safeguard for these businesses, the ones which have thought ahead will at least be aware of the dangers of putting all their eggs in one basket, and should have considered alternative strategies on which to fall back if the project does not provide the desired results.

Similar problems arise where constraints to the development – or the continuance – of the business have not been properly thought through. These might be financial, or concerned with factors such as the workforce, or available space or machinery.

For example, a business wins a new and lucrative contract which requires an increase in production of 40 per cent. The business is currently working close to full capacity producing 1,000 units a week, using a single machine and five employees. The proprietor understandably does not want to turn down the new contract on the grounds that the business cannot cope with the increased volume of production, which effectively represents an additional two days worth of work per week: 200 units a day are produced currently, and an extra 400 per week are required. Various options are available.

The business could purchase a further machine and increase the workforce. However, this option would not be efficient, given that the machine would lie idle for three out of every five days at current order levels. Further orders would have to be won to justify the additional costs. If this could be achieved, careful calculation would still be required to ensure that the considerable increase in running costs would be covered by the increased level of sales. In addition, can the business afford the capital outlay or the monthly repayments for the new machine? The only means of assessing this option is to set down in writing the projected income and costs, and cash inflows and outflows: this area is covered in chapter 4.

A second option might be to introduce a new shift of production staff, perhaps working in the evening, to meet the higher order levels. This would certainly be a cheaper option, but, again, the likely costs of extra staff and the increased running costs would need to be assessed in relation to the additional income generated.

A third – and risky – option would be to continue with the existing staff and hope that the new orders could be met by overtime work and by stalling existing customers if production fell behind schedule. The obvious dangers of this option are that although additional costs are kept to a minimum, customers are lost through an inability to satisfy orders on time and the workforce becomes dissatisfied, in spite of the financial rewards, by a rigid necessity for overtime work.

Whichever option is selected – and others may be found – the decision *must* be the result of a properly considered assessment of the advantages and risks of all the available choices. The proprietor who blindly assumed that option three would suffice without first consulting staff would be likely to find that the lack of careful consideration of the obvious constraints would quickly lead to both unhappy staff and customers.

A quite different problem arose for a rock band which found itself the victim of a very serious constraint – the loss of their lead singer, a month before Christmas, as a result of a badly broken leg. It was estimated that he would not be fit to work for some three months. Although other members of the band were capable, to a large extent, of filling his role, the act would not be the one they were contracted to stage and this option was therefore not acceptable. The same applied to the option of using a replacement singer, which had been considered as a serious possibility. Given that the band relied on the Christmas period for a substantial proportion of their bookings, the loss of their lead singer was disastrous and represented a major loss of earnings for all of the band members. Although this particular misfortune could not have been predicted, the band bitterly regretted that no insurance had been taken out to cover this sort of accident and the resulting loss of income: this had been seen as a cost saving.

This was not so much a lack of response to a constraint as a complete inability either to respond to the circumstances (because of the nature of the contracts) or to limit the financial losses suffered. The consequences were far-reaching, in that not only were immediate bookings lost at a crucial point in the entertainment season, but chances of repeat bookings at these venues in the future were damaged. In this case, the band's manager should (arguably) have insisted on resisting the temptation to make short-term financial savings, and taken a broader view of the possible consequences.

There are, however, circumstances in which the appropriate response to a change or constraint will not be easily discernible, because the power to take far-reaching decisions no longer rests with the business owner or manager.

This proved to be the case for a family-owned company which had grown over a period of ten years to become a highly profitable and financially stable concern. The business was approached with a view to acquisition by a group of companies which operated in the same field, and which was quoted on the Unlisted Securities Market. Eventually, the takeover proceeded. In spite of qualms about the inevitable loss of control which would result, the managing director felt it would be to the benefit of the company, which could not easily grow and develop further in its small and privately-owned form.

The managing director's qualms proved to be well founded: although he took on an active role on the group's main board of directors, he became increasingly frustrated at what he regarded as the excessively bureaucratic style of management by the group. What had previously been a closely controlled and tightly run company became adversely affected (in his view) by group decisions. The performance of the group overall declined, and the quoted share price fell accordingly – although his own company continued to perform well in increasingly difficult economic conditions. As the former driving force behind the company, two years later he felt that its sale, which had seemed the most beneficial long-term option, had been the wrong decision. However, the group was reluctant to sell the company back to the family since it was continuing to make a significant contribution to group profits.

A decision which had been discussed at length, and taken with the best interests of the company in mind, had ultimately proved to be the wrong one, and in the short term at least, it seemed to be irreversible. The takeover had imposed on the company constraints which the managing director and employees alike found difficult to accept, but over which they now had little control.

It is difficult to find any straightforward solution to this problem. The managing director, fully backed by the company's employees, continues to assert that he would like to return to running a privately-owned concern, but has accepted that this goal must now be regarded as a long-term aim. On the positive side, he feels the experience he has gained with the group has given him a broader outlook on business management – but it has also confirmed his suspicions that he operates most effectively in a smaller business.

It will never be possible for a business to predict or take into account every event which could have a significant adverse effect on trading or stability. However, a combination of experience and common sense should mean that the business owner or manager can identify the more obvious problems which might arise. Awareness alone of these problems is probably the most important point here, so that if it is decided to take risks, then at least the consequences will not come as a shock if the desired results are not achieved.

## Lack of defined management role / responsibility

This might initially seem to be a potential problem for larger businesses, where there are a number of tiers of management with specific roles and reporting requirements; i.e. the team leader reports to the assistant manager, who reports to the manager, who reports to the divisional director, who reports to the main board of directors. Within such a structure, it is essential for all parties to be aware of their own responsibilities and duties, and these are likely to be clearly defined.

Conversely, in the smallest business, the business owner or manager may cover a huge range of roles, dealing with sales, purchases, finance, advertising, marketing and so on. However, the majority of businesses fall somewhere between the two. The main problem for smaller businesses is that they are often too small to justify employing the level of management expertise which could bring significant benefits to the business. Those managing the business are therefore required to exhibit a high degree of versatility, as well as a high degree of competence in areas in which they are not technically trained.

Where a smaller business is essentially managed by two or three individuals, there is a danger that their roles are rather blurred and ill-defined. Whoever is in the office deals with the issues or problems which arise, rather than being able to refer them to the manager who has specific responsibility for that area of the business. It would be unrealistic to claim that there is any reason for this other than necessity in many small businesses. However, it is important for those managers to be aware of the limitations of their abilities, and to have the common sense to call on expert help when it is obviously needed. They might see this as leading to an unjustifiable level of extra costs to the business, but this needs to be assessed in terms of the additional profits which can be generated by freeing management time.

A highly successful example of this type of management was demonstrated by a small company which sold reconditioned machinery to tool-makers. The company had two directors, although only one took an active role in the company, and there were no other employees. This meant that only one individual took responsibility for the management of all functions within the company. Given that this director spent a substantial proportion of his time abroad both purchasing and selling machines, this would seem to be an impossible task. However, as a result of skilled planning and the use of external help, it was achieved, and the company was financially both profitable and stable.

The director was highly trained in the operation of the machines and had also developed successful purchasing and selling skills. Apart from this, he had little experience in business management. However, he recognized this fact and took the decision early in the life of the company to use external support to assist him, rather than to try to fulfil all roles himself. This support included self-employed technicians to recondition, repair and install machines, a specialist to provide training in the operation of the machines to customers, and a management accountant to maintain and file all accounting records and to provide monthly management reports, as well as ad hoc administrative support to keep paperwork under control.

Although he could theoretically have performed all of these tasks himself, and could have avoided the extra costs to the business by choosing this option, the additional sales he was able to generate more than compensated for the additional expenses. Furthermore, he could be satisfied that all of these tasks were carried out properly, rather than trying to be a jack of all trades himself. Equally importantly, the impression given to customers was of a well-run and high quality business – which indeed it was. In fact, this business was so successful that the director was head-hunted by a competitor, a much larger international group of companies, and offered the role of managing director of their UK operation.

The attitude to business management exemplified by this director also avoided another trap into which small and particularly family-owned businesses are apt to fall. A restricted outlook, often resulting from the fear of loss of control is a common feature of such businesses. Those in control of the business may well fail to see the need for some form of management organization and attempt to manage on a purely day-to-day basis, with little or no thought for the future development of the business – on which its survival may depend. This does not mean that a rigid structure needs to be imposed, or that individuals should be pigeon-holed into strict roles. However, it is important for all those involved in the business to have a sense of purpose in its development.

As is the case with some of the other aspects of management style discussed, a lack of definition in management role and responsibilities will not in itself cause a decline in business performance. However, where a small business is run by, say, two or three individuals, consideration given to the particular skills of those managers and the way they can best be utilized within the business will bring positive benefits. A rather hazy notion that everybody should simply devote themselves to the most urgent task of the moment is unlikely to bring the best results although, of course, there will be instances where roles overlap.

## Poor communication

It is essential for the manager or owner of a small business to be able to communicate effectively, both within the business and with external parties such as customers, suppliers and providers of finance. The skill is equally important within larger organizations, of course, but will be shared among a greater number of individuals. The small business manager will be required to communicate effectively on all levels, from straightforward dealings with employees on a day-to-day basis, to more sophisticated negotiations with, say, bankers or solicitors. There is a need to wear a number of different hats at the same time, and to be able to switch from one to another at the appropriate moment.

However good the overall quality of communication in a business, there will probably still be instances where this breaks down, whether this is directly the responsibility of the business owner or not. The consequences are, however, likely to be less serious where communication is generally good than where it is generally poor.

Poor communication can be defined in various ways, and each form will have a detrimental effect on the business. Broadly, these can be described as a lack of communication and an inability to communicate effectively.

A lack of communication can arise from ignorance, where the business owner or manager has not yet grasped what information is required by parties within and outside the business for it to run as smoothly as possible.

> The owner of a small manufacturing business decided to implement cuts in selling prices as the best solution to increased competition in their market. This meant that economies had to be achieved in the business's overheads in order to maintain a reasonable level of profitability. The business owner decided to freeze wages, amongst other measures, to keep the level of overheads as low as possible. However, he did not communicate this rationale to his employees. While they were aware that the business was in danger of suffering from increased competition, they were not aware of his proposed strategy for maintaining the business's market share. Understandably, the announcement of the pay freeze – with little explanation beyond a claim that this was due to the state of the economy – engendered considerable bad feeling in the workforce.

If, on the other hand the business owner had explained the specific problem facing the business and the fact that redundancies would otherwise have to be made, the reaction might have been far more positive. The business owner had become so embroiled in the immediate problems of the business that he had completely overlooked his role as the provider of motivation to his workforce.

A lack of communication can also be the result of a deliberate policy to reveal as little information as possible. This is often a distinguishing feature of an autocratic business owner or manager, who believes that this policy prevents others from gaining any control in the business. In fact, as in the case described above, this type of policy is more likely to lead to a dissatisfied workforce than to yield any form of positive results. While it is not necessary, and probably not practical, for all employees to have detailed knowledge of all aspects of the business, a sense that they are treated as an important asset to the business and kept informed of significant developments – either positive or negative – is a constructive way of enhancing motivation and morale. Treatment of a workforce merely as a tool – in much the same way as a piece of machinery might be treated – is hardly likely to encourage loyalty or increased involvement in the business, and in a small business this can make a vast difference.

A head-in-the-sand attitude to business management can also manifest itself in poor communication. This attitude tends to be present where the business owner or manager is relatively in-experienced, and hopes that problems will somehow disappear if they are ignored. In practical terms, this can mean, for example, that phone calls are not returned if it is suspected that a problem exists. For example, the bank manager phones to point out that the business's overdraft limit has been exceeded, but is told that the business owner is 'in a meeting'. The result is that cheques will not be honoured until the situation is rectified. The business owner is not aware of this: the phone call is not returned for fear of the consequences. In fact, discussion with the bank manager to explain that a substantial cheque from a customer has arrived late, but will clear the excess overdraft, might mean that the bank agrees to honour the business's cheque payments after all. Instead, suppliers will also become irate at the bounced cheques, and the business will lose a certain amount of goodwill both with its bank and its suppliers as a result of a situation which could easily have been avoided.

It is probably true to say that, in most circumstances, good communication breeds good communication. If a business owner or manager leads by example, there is a far greater probability that both staff and the third parties with whom the business deals will respond positively. This does not imply taking an ingratiating approach to management, but developing and maintaining an awareness of the needs of individuals and the business.

> A partnership servicing and repairing industrial machinery, which employed two technicians, managed to achieve this largely as a result of the example set by the most senior of the three partners. He had developed a very open management style, which included ensuring that he and his colleagues met regularly to discuss any aspects of the business which required particular attention, and all of them felt able to express their views on decisions which affected the future of the business. The business progressed smoothly under this style of management which encouraged maximum involvement in both day-to-day matters and broader strategic issues. Given that the two technicians and one of the partners spent little time at their office base, the quality of communication achieved was surprisingly high.

Of course, this type of tight-knit team will not be practicable in all types of business, but it nonetheless serves as a useful model. When employees spend most of their time visiting customers or clients, it is particularly important to ensure that time is regularly set aside to meet, even if only briefly, say on a Monday morning, to discuss any significant issues which require resolution.

## Conclusions

All individuals develop their own management style, although in larger organizations this might be shaped by training specifically designed to reflect the policies of that organization. A smaller business whose owner or manager relies more on experience and intuition than formal training does not need to be at a disadvantage. However, the range of roles fulfilled by a manager under these circumstances makes it a function whose complexities should not be underestimated. The pitfalls and difficulties described above are amongst some of the more common experienced by owners and managers of small businesses and amongst the ones whose consequences can be most serious. There are, of course, many others, some of which will be specific to certain types of business. However, the sensible and forward-thinking manager will remain open to the fact that new problems can always arise and above all, he or she will not fall into the trap of refusing to acknowledge their existence.

## 4. Financial planning

Larger well-managed businesses tend to go through fairly detailed and rigorous planning procedures, which usually incorporate strategic plans, financial projections and more detailed departmental budgets. Each of the three stages of the planning process will flow logically from the previous stage, and overall the plan will encapsulate the trading and financial decisions and expectations of the business for the short- and medium-term future.

In smaller businesses, the process tends to be carried out on a far more piecemeal basis, or in response to a specific need, such as securing additional loan finance from a bank or evaluating the likely results of opening a new branch or office. As a result, plans for the future tend to be rather vague and are often simply contained within the mind of the business owner.

This tends to be particularly true during periods of economic recession, when many smaller businesses are more concerned with day-to-day survival than with planning for a future which looks increasingly uncertain. Equally, in more favourable conditions, there may seem little immediate need for formal planning if business appears to be progressing satisfactorily. There may be a temptation, during an economic upturn, to feel that business performance is bound to improve as the economy picks up. Some business owners and managers may argue that there is little point in spending valuable time on an exercise which seems largely academic.

## Why is planning important?

A business which does not prepare formal plans or financial projections for internal use is not necessarily one which is more likely to fail. However, lack of planning is often symptomatic of an overall lack of financial control, which frequently stems from a perceived shortage of available time and resources to devote to such matters. Many smaller businesses tend to be sales driven; perhaps understandably, it is felt that satisfying existing customers and increasing the customer base takes precedence over all other business matters.

Of course, financial planning alone will not lead to the survival of a failing business. However, it can contribute significantly to an improved degree of awareness of and control over the financial management of the business, if those responsible for decision-making choose to use the process as an additional management tool.

Setting down plans and expectations in writing is the most effective means of focusing the mind on the future of the business, and does not need to be a time-consuming exercise. It should also provide the business owner or manager with a better feel for business performance. If unexpected events do subsequently arise – either positive or negative – then their impact on the business overall will be far more readily assessable than if the business had no clear idea of trading expectations.

> For example, a business hiring out catering equipment for corporate and private entertainment functions fell prey to this problem, finding that corporate demand had decreased as businesses cut back their entertaining and hospitality budgets. The proprietor had a general feeling that since a reasonable bank balance had built up, the business could continue to meet its payments for overhead expenditure at the reduced level of turnover and therefore there was no real cause for concern in the short term. However, this feeling was not quantified and, after a few months, the business was in need of overdraft facilities and had begun to stall payments to creditors. The business's bank manager was not sympathetic, having received no warning of the potential problem, and goodwill with creditors diminished fast. If the proprietor had attempted to quantify the effect on the profit and loss account and bank account, warned its bank and tried to negotiate more favourable terms with creditors, the story would probably have been a different one – and the business might have survived.

A large number of small businesses have been set up in recent years as a direct result of redundancy. Redundancy settlements are used to finance capital expenditure and provide working capital. For many individuals, where the chances of securing employment are slim, setting up in business seems a positive move, and indeed their aims are very positive ones. In these circumstances, financial planning is vital, particularly where the individual has little or no previous business management experience, which is often the case.

As with existing businesses, such individuals will probably have a general idea of their goals, of how they propose to develop a customer base and of some of the costs of running the business in its early stages. It is less likely that this information will be written down and assessed *before* action is taken and money spent to set up the business. The decision to start a business is a huge step to take, and it is vital to spend time quantifying whether it has a chance of financial survival. Far too many failures occur in the very early stages because it quickly emerges that cash is running out before the business has got off the ground.

A skilled painter and decorator, made redundant from a medium-sized company, discovered this painful fact the hard way. Having used more of his redundancy settlement than he had planned to purchase a new van and additional equipment, he hoped to secure work via local advertising and personal recommendations.

Unfortunately, a regular flow of work proved far more difficult to achieve than he had expected. Although the costs of running the business were not great, he also found that he was charging less for his work than he had imagined, in order not to lose customers to his competitors. The remainder of his redundancy settlement was being used to contribute to domestic expenditure, since the business was simply not generating sufficient cash, and these savings dwindled fast.

He decided that he had little option but to continue with his business, while searching for employment. However, he would now advise individuals in his circumstances to think hard, plan ahead and use whatever sources of advice they can before setting up in business.

Local enterprise agencies and business advisory offices are usually happy to provide guidance in the form of consultation and / or literature to individuals who are considering setting up a business, and their resources should not be ignored.

The process of preparing business plans, projections and budgets is one which is still frequently regarded with cynicism by smaller businesses. However, it should always be remembered that whether the plans are prepared for internal or external purposes, they should ultimately be used to the benefit of the business, not the bank manager or accountant! A bank manager or accountant may make decisions about future lending or offer advice based on the plans, but the most important users of plans are those responsible for the running of the business.

## The planning process

Business plans may be prepared because they are required by a third party – by a bank to support an application for overdraft or loan finance, for example – or purely for internal use within the business.

In both cases, the overall aim of business planning is to assess future expected business performance, to set realistic goals for the future and to determine whether the resources are available to achieve those goals. Later on, the plans can be used to monitor business performance. The process should also focus attention on potential areas of strength and weakness, so that these can be exploited or remedied.

For internal use, it is most common – and useful – to prepare a projected profit and loss account, cashflow and balance sheet. For most smaller businesses, these will cover a twelve-month period which ties up with the accounting year-end. Each of the three elements of the projections should be backed up by written assumptions, and more detailed working papers if necessary.

The mechanics of preparing integrated projections – i.e. where the profit and loss account, cashflow and balance sheet are linked together – are not difficult, but do demand a reasonable level of accounting knowledge. Computer spreadsheet software is ideal for this exercise, and it is usually a good idea for an accountant to be involved if this type of projection is required. 'Standard' computer models for business planning and projections are available and are becoming increasingly numerous; but do be cautious about investing in such software unless you are absolutely sure it is suitable for your business. Remember that businesses themselves are very rarely 'standard'.

Less complex plans covering a profit and loss account and cashflow can be prepared manually, although the calculation of an accurate balance sheet will be more tricky.

The process might seem daunting, but it is well worth spending a few hours setting down in writing estimates for future business performance. It does require care; projections which are drawn up on false or over-optimistic assumptions will benefit nobody. However, preparing a simple projected profit and loss account and cashflow is always a useful exercise in focusing attention on a business's future.

## Simple financial projections: an example

The planning process is based on asking questions, and a good starting point for an existing business is the most recent set of annual accounts. The example below illustrates a small business which had experienced several difficult years of trading and felt it needed to exercise tighter financial control over both direct and indirect costs in an attempt to return the company to profitability. The company's bankers were exerting increasing pressure for the bank overdraft to be reduced, and also encouraged the preparation of projections to focus the managing director's attention on the company's financial and trading position.

The projections were based on the following broad assumptions. It should be stressed that if these were to be presented to a bank, for example, they would need to be set out in more detail.

1 Sales for the first seven months would remain at the same level

as the previous year, although the company believed a 15 per cent increase could easily be achieved. For the last five months, an increase of £10,000 per month was included, representing a new and regular contract which had already been agreed and finalized.

2 Cost of sales was estimated at 75 per cent of sales, compared

## Fine Freight Limited – Profit and Loss Account

|  | *31 August 1992* |  | *31 August 1991* |
|---|---|---|---|
| Sales |  | 425,319 | 579,777 |
| Cost of sales |  | 331,264 | 516,081 |
| Gross profit |  | 94,055 | 63,696 |
| Gross profit % | 22.11 | 10.99 | |
| | | | |
| *Overheads* | | | |
| Salaries | 34,250 | | 59,307 |
| Telephone | 8,915 | | 15,959 |
| Light, heat and power | 350 | | 310 |
| Rent, rates and insurance | 8,463 | | 11,171 |
| Motor expenses | 4,749 | | 10,717 |
| Postage and stationery | 1,465 | | 3,359 |
| Professional charges | 5,577 | | 5,814 |
| Advertising and marketing | 4,472 | | 2,894 |
| Lease of fax | 1,393 | | 604 |
| Entertaining | 1,728 | | 2,436 |
| Sundry expenses | 988 | | 3,259 |
| Bank charges | 1,954 | | 2,346 |
| Bank interest | 3,031 | | 7,649 |
| Hire purchase interest | 553 | | 591 |
| Depreciation | 5,780 | | 12,642 |
| Bad debts written off | 15,724 | | 3,788 |
| | | 99,392 | 142,846 |
| Net loss | | £(5,337) | £(79,150) |

with 78 per cent in the previous year. This improvement was the result of successful negotiations with a major supplier, who was eager to retain the company's custom in the face of competition from alternative suppliers who had been contacted by the company.

3 Overheads are based largely on the totals for the prior year, with an allowance for inflation. It should be possible to estimate most items with reasonable accuracy, in particular overheads such as rent or lease of equipment. It has been agreed that there will be no salary increases throughout the year.

4 Receipts from customers and payments to suppliers are both based on credit periods of 60 days. Overhead payments are allocated on the basis of known payment cycles wherever possible, or in the month in which the expense is incurred.

5 The company suffered from bad debts in the previous year, but is confident that improved credit checks and credit control will largely overcome the problem in this period.

The company prepared a projected profit and loss account and cashflow, and used as their starting point the financial statements for the two previous years, which are set out opposite.

The projected results show a marked improvement over the previous two years, and for this reason should be treated with healthy caution. They may well be based on reasonable assumptions, but a turnaround from a net loss of £5,337 shown by the prior year's accounts to a net profit before tax of some £34,000 in the projected profit and loss account is a substantial achievement in difficult trading conditions. The same applies to the improvement in the bank balance shown by the cashflow projection from an overdraft of almost £34,000 at the beginning of the year to a positive balance of over £3,500 twelve months later. Is this realistic, or has the managing director been over-optimistic in his expectations?

Having set down what it believes to be the most likely results for the year ahead, the company should also consider performing sensitivity analysis on its projections. This means asking a series

# Fine Freight Limited – Projected Profit and Loss Account

| | Sep 92 | Oct 92 | Nov 92 | Dec 92 | Jan 93 | Feb 93 |
|---|---|---|---|---|---|---|
| Sales | 35,500 | 35,500 | 35,500 | 35,500 | 35,500 | 35,500 |
| Cost of sales | 26,625 | 26,625 | 26,625 | 26,625 | 26,625 | 26,625 |
| **Gross profit** | **8,875** | **8,875** | **8,875** | **8,875** | **8,875** | **8,875** |
| **Gross profit %** | **25** | **25** | **25** | **25** | **25** | **25** |
| Overheads | | | | | | |
| *Salaries* | 2,875 | 2,875 | 2,875 | 2,875 | 2,875 | 2,875 |
| *Telephone* | 792 | 792 | 792 | 792 | 792 | 792 |
| *Light, heat and power* | 79 | 79 | 79 | 79 | 79 | 79 |
| *Rent, rates and insurance* | 729 | 729 | 729 | 729 | 729 | 729 |
| *Motor expenses* | 417 | 417 | 417 | 417 | 417 | 417 |
| *Postage and stationery* | 125 | 125 | 125 | 125 | 125 | 125 |
| *Professional charges* | | | 1,500 | | | 1,500 |
| *Advertising and marketing* | 1,600 | 100 | 100 | 100 | 100 | 100 |
| *Lease of fax* | 125 | 125 | 125 | 125 | 125 | 125 |
| *Entertaining* | 150 | 150 | 150 | 150 | 150 | 150 |
| *Sundry expenses* | 100 | 100 | 100 | 100 | 100 | 100 |
| *Bank charges* | 375 | | | 375 | | |
| *Bank interest* | 302 | 239 | 210 | 229 | 177 | 148 |
| *Hire purchase interest* | 42 | 42 | 42 | 42 | 42 | 42 |
| *Depreciation* | 417 | 417 | 417 | 417 | 417 | 417 |
| *Bad debt provision* | 1,500 | | | | | |
| | **9,627** | **6,189** | **7,660** | **6,554** | **6,127** | **7,598** |
| **Net profit / (loss)** | (752) | 2,686 | 1,215 | 2,321 | 2,748 | 1,277 |

**Note:** All amounts are expressed to the nearest £1. Small rounding differences will

| Mar 93 | Apr 93 | May 93 | Jun 93 | Jul 93 | Aug 93 | Total |
|---|---|---|---|---|---|---|
| 35,500 | 45,500 | 45,500 | 45,500 | 45,500 | 45,500 | 476,000 |
| 26,625 | 34,125 | 34,125 | 34,125 | 34,125 | 34,125 | 357,000 |
| **8,875** | **11,375** | **11,375** | **11,375** | **11,375** | **11,375** | **119,000** |
| 25 | 25 | 25 | 25 | 25 | 25 | 25 |
| | | | | | | |
| 2,875 | 2,875 | 2,875 | 2,875 | 2,875 | 2,875 | 34,500 |
| 792 | 792 | 792 | 792 | 792 | 792 | 9,500 |
| 79 | 79 | 79 | 79 | 79 | 79 | 950 |
| 729 | 729 | 729 | 729 | 729 | 729 | 8,750 |
| 417 | 417 | 417 | 417 | 417 | 417 | 5,000 |
| 125 | 125 | 125 | 125 | 125 | 125 | 1,500 |
| | | 1,500 | | | 1,500 | 6,000 |
| 1,600 | 100 | 100 | 100 | 100 | 100 | 4,200 |
| 125 | 125 | 125 | 125 | 125 | 125 | 1,500 |
| 150 | 150 | 150 | 150 | 150 | 150 | 1,800 |
| 100 | 100 | 100 | 100 | 100 | 100 | 1,200 |
| 375 | | | 375 | | | 1,500 |
| 182 | 131 | 102 | 99 | 22 | 0 | 1,841 |
| 42 | 42 | 42 | 42 | 42 | 42 | 500 |
| 417 | 417 | 417 | 417 | 417 | 417 | 5,000 |
| | | | | | | 1,500 |
| **8,007** | **6,081** | **7,552** | **6,424** | **5,972** | **7,450** | **85,241** |
| 868 | 5,294 | 3,823 | 4,951 | 5,403 | 3,925 | 33,759 |

therefore arise in totals.

# Fine Freight Limited – projected cashflow

| | Sep 92 | Oct 92 | Nov 92 | Dec 92 | Jan 93 | Feb 93 |
|---|---|---|---|---|---|---|
| *Receipts opening debtors* | 40,148 | 40,148 | | | | |
| *Receipts sales* | | | 41,713 | 41,713 | 41,713 | 41,713 |
| *Other income* | | | | | | |
| **Total receipts** | **40,148** | **40,148** | **41,713** | **41,713** | **41,713** | **41,713** |
| *Payments to opening creditors* | 28,435 | 28,435 | | | | |
| *Payments cost of sales* | | | 31,284 | 31,284 | 31,284 | 31,284 |
| *Salaries* | 1,978 | 1,978 | 1,978 | 1,978 | 1,978 | 1,978 |
| PAYE/NIC | 897 | 897 | 897 | 897 | 897 | 897 |
| *Telephone* | | | 2,791 | | | 2,791 |
| *Light, heat and power* | | 238 | | | 238 | |
| *Rent, rates and insurance* | 2,104 | 42 | 42 | 2,104 | 42 | 42 |
| *Motor expenses* | 490 | 490 | 490 | 490 | 490 | 490 |
| *Postage and stationery* | 147 | 147 | 147 | 147 | 147 | 147 |
| *Professional charges* | | | | 1,763 | | |
| *Advertising and marketing* | 1,880 | 118 | 118 | 118 | 118 | 118 |
| *Lease of fax* | 147 | 147 | 147 | 147 | 147 | 147 |
| *Entertaining* | 150 | 150 | 150 | 150 | 150 | 150 |
| *Sundry expenses* | 100 | 100 | 100 | 100 | 100 | 100 |
| *Bank charges* | 375 | | | 375 | | |
| *Bank interest* | 650 | | | 751 | | |
| *Hire purchase payments* | 230 | 230 | 230 | 230 | 230 | 230 |
| *VAT* | 3,200 | | | 3,316 | | |
| **Total payments** | **40,783** | **32,970** | **38,373** | **43,849** | **35,819** | **38,373** |
| *Opening bank balance* | (33,871) | (34,506) | (27,329) | (23,989) | (26,125) | (20,232) |
| *Net movement* | (635) | 7,178 | 3,340 | (2,137) | 5,893 | 3,340 |
| **Closing bank balance** | **(34,506)** | **(27,329)** | **(23,989)** | **(26,125)** | **(20,232)** | **(16,892)** |

| Mar 93 | Apr 93 | May 93 | Jun 93 | Jul 93 | Aug 93 | Total |
|---|---|---|---|---|---|---|
| | | | | | | 80,295 |
| 41,713 | 41,713 | 41,713 | 53,463 | 53,463 | 53,463 | 452,375 |
| | | | | | | 0 |
| **41,713** | **41,713** | **41,713** | **53,463** | **53,463** | **53,463** | **532,670** |
| | | | | | | 56,870 |
| 31,284 | 31,284 | 31,284 | 40,097 | 40,097 | 40,097 | 339,281 |
| 1,978 | 1,978 | 1,978 | 1,978 | 1,978 | 1,978 | 23,739 |
| 897 | 897 | 897 | 897 | 897 | 897 | 10,761 |
| | | 2,791 | | | 2,791 | 11,163 |
| | 238 | | | 238 | | 950 |
| 2,104 | 42 | 42 | 2,104 | 42 | 42 | 8,750 |
| 490 | 490 | 490 | 490 | 490 | 490 | 5,875 |
| 147 | 147 | 147 | 147 | 147 | 147 | 1,763 |
| 1,763 | | | 1,763 | | | 5,288 |
| 1,880 | 118 | 118 | 118 | 118 | 118 | 4,935 |
| 147 | 147 | 147 | 147 | 147 | 147 | 1,763 |
| 150 | 150 | 150 | 150 | 150 | 150 | 1,800 |
| 100 | 100 | 100 | 100 | 100 | 100 | 1,200 |
| 375 | | | 375 | | | 1,500 |
| 553 | | | 415 | | | 2,369 |
| 230 | 230 | 230 | 230 | 230 | 230 | 2,760 |
| 3,579 | | | 4,191 | | | 14,286 |
| **45,677** | **35,819** | **38,373** | **53,201** | **44,632** | **47,185** | **495,052** |
| (16,892) | (20,856) | (14,963) | (11,623) | (11,361) | (2,530) | (33,871) |
| (3,964) | 5,893 | 3,340 | 262 | 8,831 | 6,278 | 37,618 |
| **(20,856)** | **(14,963)** | **(11,623)** | **(11,361)** | **(2,530)** | **3,747** | **3,747** |

of 'What if. . . ?' questions, to determine the likely outcome if trading does not proceed according to plan.

## WHAT IF SALES FALL SHORT OF TARGET BY 20 PER CENT?

The effect on the profit and loss account is:

| | |
|---|---:|
| Total sales | £476,000 |
| Less : 20% | 95,200 |
| Revised sales | 380,800 |
| Revised cost of sales (75%) | 285,600 |
| Revised gross profit | **£ 95,200** |

Gross profit, although reduced by £24,000, still covers the projected overheads of £85,627, although it should be remembered that bank charges and interest are likely to be higher at the revised level of sales.

The effect on the bank overdraft would be more serious. Although there is a delay of two months before the receipts and payments affect the cashflow, and therefore only ten months' worth of the effect is felt in the current year, the impact on the bank balance is obviously a negative one.

## WHAT IF COST OF SALES INCREASES TO 85 PER CENT?

| | |
|---|---:|
| Total sales | £476,000 |
| Revised cost of sales (85%) | 404,600 |
| Revised gross profit | **£ 71,400** |

The increase would be disastrous. Gross profit decreases by £47,600 and also falls short of projected overheads by £13,841 – and, again, bank charges and interest would probably increase.

The effect on cashflow would be equally disastrous, with an increase in the bank overdraft at the end of the year, rather than the projected achievement of a positive bank balance.

## WHAT IF 50 PER CENT OF CUSTOMERS TAKE 90 DAYS TO PAY INSTEAD OF THE AGREED 60 DAYS?

As a rough guide, this would mean that some £20,000 would be received one month later, until month ten, when this increases to over £26,000. Again the effect on the bank account is serious, with the company still showing a large overdraft at the end of the year.

The list of questions which can be asked is almost endless. What if the 'firm' contract which is due to come into operation in month eight does not after all materialize? What if new or replacement equipment is required? While it is not necessary to present the most pessimistic outlook in financial projections, these questions *must* be asked in order to gain a grasp of the impact that unexpected events could have on trading for the year ahead.

In addition, these are exactly the questions that a bank manager or adviser would ask in assessing the future prospects of the company, and the answers must therefore have been considered in advance. While projections will never be automatically 'right', their purpose is to construct a realistic picture of likely events in the short-term future. For example, the reduction in the bank overdraft throughout the year, while a very positive goal, is likely to attract a sceptical response from an external observer. Can an improvement of over £37,000 in the bank balance really be achieved in a twelve-month period, given difficult trading conditions? Can sales really be held at the previous year's level? Will there really be only £1,500 of bad debts this year, compared with over £15,000 last year?

The balance between presenting a pessimistic and realistic outlook is a fine one, and to some degree must depend upon general economic conditions as well. Although the improvement in this company's last 'actual' results compared with the previous year is significant, there is no guarantee that the improvement will continue.

The second scenario for this company excludes the 'firm' contract, due to begin in month eight, and reduces the projected gross margin in the profit and loss account from 25 per cent to 20 per cent. The effect is to reduce the projected profit for the year of

# Fine Freight Limited – Projected Profit and Loss Account

|  | Sep 92 | Oct 92 | Nov 92 | Dec 92 | Jan 93 | Feb 93 |
|---|---|---|---|---|---|---|
| Sales | 35,500 | 35,500 | 35,500 | 35,500 | 35,500 | 35,500 |
| Cost of sales | 28,400 | 28,400 | 28,400 | 28,400 | 28,400 | 28,400 |
| **Gross profit** | **7,100** | **7,100** | **7,100** | **7,100** | **7,100** | **7,100** |
| **Gross profit %** | **20** | **20** | **20** | **20** | **20** | **20** |
| Overheads |  |  |  |  |  |  |
| *Salaries* | 2,875 | 2,875 | 2,875 | 2,875 | 2,875 | 2,875 |
| *Telephone* | 792 | 792 | 792 | 792 | 792 | 792 |
| *Light, heat and power* | 79 | 79 | 79 | 79 | 79 | 79 |
| *Rent, rates and insurance* | 729 | 729 | 729 | 729 | 729 | 729 |
| *Motor expenses* | 417 | 417 | 417 | 417 | 417 | 417 |
| *Postage and stationery* | 125 | 125 | 125 | 125 | 125 | 125 |
| *Professional charges* |  |  | 1,500 |  |  | 1,500 |
| *Advertising and marketing* | 1,600 | 100 | 100 | 100 | 100 | 100 |
| *Lease of fax* | 125 | 125 | 125 | 125 | 125 | 125 |
| *Entertaining* | 150 | 150 | 150 | 150 | 150 | 150 |
| *Sundry expenses* | 100 | 100 | 100 | 100 | 100 | 100 |
| *Bank charges* | 375 |  |  | 375 |  |  |
| *Bank interest* | 302 | 239 | 228 | 257 | 224 | 213 |
| *Hire purchase interest* | 42 | 42 | 42 | 42 | 42 | 42 |
| *Depreciation* | 417 | 417 | 417 | 417 | 417 | 417 |
| *Bad debt provision* | 1,500 |  |  |  |  |  |
|  | **9,627** | **6,189** | **7,678** | **6,582** | **6,174** | **7,663** |
| **Net profit / (loss)** | (2,527) | 911 | (578) | 518 | 926 | (563) |

| | Mar 93 | Apr 93 | May 93 | Jun 93 | Jul 93 | Aug 93 | Total |
|---|---|---|---|---|---|---|---|
| | 35,500 | 35,500 | 35,500 | 35,500 | 35,500 | 35,500 | 426,000 |
| | 28,400 | 28,400 | 28,400 | 28,400 | 28,400 | 28,400 | 340,800 |
| | **7,100** | **7,100** | **7,100** | **7,100** | **7,100** | **7,100** | **85,200** |
| | 20 | 20 | 20 | 20 | 20 | 20 | 20 |
| | | | | | | | |
| | 2,875 | 2,875 | 2,875 | 2,875 | 2,875 | 2,875 | 34,500 |
| | 792 | 792 | 792 | 792 | 792 | 792 | 9,500 |
| | 79 | 79 | 79 | 79 | 79 | 79 | 950 |
| | 729 | 729 | 729 | 729 | 729 | 729 | 8,750 |
| | 417 | 417 | 417 | 417 | 417 | 417 | 5,000 |
| | 125 | 125 | 125 | 125 | 125 | 125 | 1,500 |
| | | | 1,500 | | | 1,500 | 6,000 |
| | 1,600 | 100 | 100 | 100 | 100 | 100 | 4,200 |
| | 125 | 125 | 125 | 125 | 125 | 125 | 1,500 |
| | 150 | 150 | 150 | 150 | 150 | 150 | 1,800 |
| | 100 | 100 | 100 | 100 | 100 | 100 | 1,200 |
| | 375 | | | 375 | | | 1,500 |
| | 259 | 225 | 215 | 243 | 210 | 199 | 2,813 |
| | 42 | 42 | 42 | 42 | 42 | 42 | 500 |
| | 417 | 417 | 417 | 417 | 417 | 417 | 5,000 |
| | | | | | | | 1,500 |
| | **8,084** | **6,175** | **7,665** | **6,568** | **6,160** | **7,649** | **86,213** |
| | (984) | 925 | (565) | 532 | 940 | (549) | (1,013) |

# Fine Freight Limited – projected cashflow

| | Sep 92 | Oct 92 | Nov 92 | Dec 92 | Jan 93 | Feb 93 |
|---|---|---|---|---|---|---|
| *Receipts opening debtors* | 40,148 | 40,148 | | | | |
| *Receipts sales* | | | 41,713 | 41,713 | 41,713 | 41,713 |
| *Other income* | | | | | | |
| **Total receipts** | **40,148** | **40,148** | **41,713** | **41,713** | **41,713** | **41,713** |
| *Payments to opening creditors* | 28,435 | 28,435 | | | | |
| *Payments cost of sales* | | | 33,370 | 33,370 | 33,370 | 33,370 |
| *Salaries* | 1,978 | 1,978 | 1,978 | 1,978 | 1,978 | 1,978 |
| PAYE/NIC | 897 | 897 | 897 | 897 | 897 | 897 |
| *Telephone* | | | 2,791 | | | 2,791 |
| *Light, heat and power* | | 238 | | | 238 | |
| *Rent, rates and insurance* | 2,104 | 42 | 42 | 2,104 | 42 | 42 |
| *Motor expenses* | 490 | 490 | 490 | 490 | 490 | 490 |
| *Postage and stationery* | 147 | 147 | 147 | 147 | 147 | 147 |
| *Professional charges* | | | | 1,763 | | |
| *Advertising and marketing* | 1,880 | 118 | 118 | 118 | 118 | 118 |
| *Lease of fax* | 147 | 147 | 147 | 147 | 147 | 147 |
| *Entertaining* | 150 | 150 | 150 | 150 | 150 | 150 |
| *Sundry expenses* | 100 | 100 | 100 | 100 | 100 | 100 |
| *Bank charges* | 375 | | | 375 | | |
| *Bank interest* | 650 | | | 769 | | |
| *Hire purchase payments* | 230 | 230 | 230 | 230 | 230 | 230 |
| *VAT* | 3,200 | | | 2,384 | | |
| **Total payments** | **40,783** | **32,970** | **40,458** | **45,021** | **37,905** | **40,458** |
| *Opening bank balance* | (33,871) | (34,506) | (27,329) | (26,074) | (29,383) | (25,575) |
| *Net movement* | (635) | 7,178 | 1,254 | (3,309) | 3,808 | 1,254 |
| **Closing bank balance** | **(34,506)** | **(27,329)** | **(26,074)** | **(29,383)** | **(25,575)** | **(24,321)** |

| Mar 93 | Apr 93 | May 93 | Jun 93 | Jul 93 | Aug 93 | Total |
|---|---|---|---|---|---|---|
| | | | | | | 80,295 |
| 41,713 | 41,713 | 41,713 | 41,713 | 41,713 | 41,713 | 417,125 |
| | | | | | | 0 |
| **41,713** | **41,713** | **41,713** | **41,713** | **41,713** | **41,713** | **497,420** |
| | | | | | | 56,870 |
| 33,370 | 33,370 | 33,370 | 33,370 | 33,370 | 33,370 | 333,700 |
| 1,978 | 1,978 | 1,978 | 1,978 | 1,978 | 1,978 | 23,739 |
| 897 | 897 | 897 | 897 | 897 | 897 | 10,761 |
| | | 2,791 | | | 2,791 | 11,163 |
| | 238 | | | 238 | | 950 |
| 2,104 | 42 | 42 | 2,104 | 42 | 42 | 8,750 |
| 490 | 490 | 490 | 490 | 490 | 490 | 5,875 |
| 147 | 147 | 147 | 147 | 147 | 147 | 1,763 |
| 1,763 | | | 1,763 | | | 5,288 |
| 1,880 | 118 | 118 | 118 | 118 | 118 | 4,935 |
| 147 | 147 | 147 | 147 | 147 | 147 | 1,763 |
| 150 | 150 | 150 | 150 | 150 | 150 | 1,800 |
| 100 | 100 | 100 | 100 | 100 | 100 | 1,200 |
| 375 | | | 375 | | | 1,500 |
| 694 | | | 699 | | | 2,812 |
| 230 | 230 | 230 | 230 | 230 | 230 | 2,760 |
| 2,647 | | | 2,384 | | | 10,616 |
| **46,971** | **37,905** | **40,458** | **44,951** | **37,905** | **40,458** | **486,242** |
| (24,321) | (29,579) | (25,771) | (24,517) | (27,755) | (23,948) | (33,871) |
| (5,258) | 3,808 | 1,254 | (3,238) | 3,808 | 1,254 | 11,178 |
| **(29,579)** | **(25,771)** | **(24,517)** | **(27,755)** | **(23,948)** | **(22,693)** | **(22,693)** |

£33,759 in the original projection to a loss of £1,013. Similarly, the bank balance is reduced from a positive £3,747 at the year end in the original projection to an overdraft of £22,693. While this is still an improvement on the overdrawn balance of £33,871 at the beginning of the year, it illustrates how easy it is to be over-optimistic about future results. The first set of projections might appear realistic, but it is extremely important to assess the impact of unexpected negative events.

In this case, both versions were presented to the company's bank manager who was prepared to allow the company's existing overdraft facility to continue. Although the financial projections are fairly simple ones, they were adequate to demonstrate to the bank that the company is taking a responsible and constructive attitude to the reduction of its borrowings and, more generally, to the future of the company.

How does the business owner or manager arrive at the figures to be used in the financial projections? As mentioned above, for an existing business a good starting point is its accounts for last year. To construct a simple projected profit and loss account, the figures in the accounts for turnover, cost of sales and overheads are reassessed based on expectations for the coming year, and divided by twelve to achieve monthly estimates. If trading tends to be seasonal, then turnover should be appropriately weighted throughout the year.

## Financial projections for new businesses

For a new business, the process is inevitably more difficult, because no guidelines based on prior periods' trading will be available.

The first and probably the most difficult problem is to estimate the level of turnover the business can generate. To achieve this it is necessary to know the number of sales made and the selling price of each unit. Clearly, selling price will ultimately be affected by what customers are prepared to pay, and by reference to competitors' prices. However, the effect of changes in volumes of sales and in selling price can be calculated by applying the breakeven equation, as follows:

Breakeven point is where
Units sold × selling price    = Units sold × cost price + fixed costs

Fixed costs refer to those overhead costs which are not directly attributable to the product or service sold and which are therefore not affected by the level of sales. These will include such expenses as rent, administrative salaries, telephone costs, professional costs and so on.

If fixed costs per annum are, say, £50,000, the selling price per unit is £30 per unit and direct costs per unit are £20 per unit, the breakeven level of sales is calculated as:

$$\frac{\text{Fixed costs}}{\text{Selling price} - \text{cost price}}$$

$$= \frac{50,000}{30 - 20}$$

$$= \underline{5,000 \text{ units}}$$

Alternatively, if it is known that the maximum production capacity with the existing machinery and workforce is 4,500 units per annum, and it is required to determine the breakeven selling price, the equation can be adapted to:

Selling price × units    = Fixed costs + (units × cost price)

= 50,000 + 90,000

= $\underline{140,000}$

Selling price = $\dfrac{140,000}{4,500}$        = $\underline{£31.12}$

These calculations take no account of a target net profit before tax. If the target is, say, £15,000, this figure should be added to the fixed costs in the above calculations. In the second example, this would increase the selling price to:

$$\frac{140,000 + 15,000}{4,500} = \underline{£34.45}$$

It is rare for selling price calculations to be as simple as this in reality. It may be that the market will not bear a price in excess of £25 per unit. In this case, it would be necessary to look at reducing costs, either direct or fixed; or increasing production and / or sales; or maybe a decision would be reached not to set up the business at all.

Alternatively, price can be set by reference to the market rate or to competitors' prices. In both cases, it is absolutely vital to ensure that turnover is adequate to cover the business's costs. There is no point in building up a vast customer base by under-cutting competitors' prices if the resulting turnover is insufficient to cover costs. It is a commonly held belief, particularly when economic conditions are poor, that if turnover is increasing then profits will increase accordingly. If the increase in turnover has resulted from a cut in selling prices with no corresponding decrease in costs, then it is highly likely that the business will suffer decreasing profits, if not increasing losses.

Cost of sales should be easier to estimate, once a target level of turnover has been determined, and it will include materials, direct labour and any other costs directly attributable to sales.

It is easy to omit overhead categories. To avoid omissions, overheads should be split into 'types' for easier reference. These include:

- Distribution costs

  Transport / delivery
  Storage

- Property costs

  Rent and rates
  Service charge
  Insurance
  Electricity
  Repairs and renewals

- Administration costs

  Wages and salaries / NIC
  Telephone
  Printing, postage and stationery
  Advertising and marketing
  Motor expenses
  Travel and entertaining

- Professional costs

  Accountancy and audit
  Solicitor

- Finance costs

  Bank charges
  Bank interest
  Hire purchase interest

- Other costs            Depreciation
                                  Bad debts

The list will not cover every type of overhead, but the headings should provide an *aide-mémoire* for the majority of costs.

All items in the projected profit and loss account should be stated *net* of Value Added Tax, assuming that the business is registered for VAT.

The conversion of the projected profit and loss account into a cashflow statement is not difficult, although again the exercise is based upon assumptions as to when cash will be received from customers or paid to suppliers. The most straightforward approach is to work through the profit and loss account line by line, and estimate when cash will be paid or received. Certain payments are likely to be made monthly, for example, to trade suppliers for goods or services, whereas others will be quarterly, for example, for rent, telephone or fuel bills. All items in the cashflow should include VAT where appropriate.

It will also be necessary to include quarterly payments to HM Customs and Excise for VAT due. This should be calculated on the basis of the VAT charged for the quarter on sales less the VAT suffered on purchases of goods and services, and the estimated payment (or repayment) inserted in the appropriate month.

Bank interest should also be calculated on the closing bank balance at the end of each month, if the balance becomes negative, and the appropriate amount should also be entered in the profit and loss account for the month. The actual payment of bank interest will probably be quarterly.

Any amounts drawn out of the business by the proprietor or partners which will not be covered by wages and salaries should also be included in the projected cashflow, although these will not appear in the profit and loss account.

Other items to be included in the cashflow which do not appear in the profit and loss account might include loan repayments or receipts and purchases of fixed assets. Conversely, items which appear in the profit and loss account but not the cashflow (because there is no actual cash movement) include depreciation and the write-off of bad debts.

## Using financial projections to set goals

The purpose of preparing projections is to assess estimated future performance and to set goals for the business. While the future will always contain unknown elements there is really no other way to arrive at considered decisions for the future of the business.

For example, the managing director of Precision Metal Ltd, a company manufacturing wrought iron garden furniture, decides he wants to increase the company's existing turnover of £200,000 by 25 per cent in the coming year. His research has shown that the company's existing retail outlets could easily support the increased level of turnover. He proposes to purchase additional new equipment and to take on an additional employee to cope with the extra workload.

However, what he has not properly taken into consideration is the cost of financing the increased turnover. As well as the purchase of additional raw materials which will have to be paid for before cash is received for subsequent sales, there will be hire purchase repayments or outright cash payments for the new equipment and an additional wages cost per month. Selling prices, on the other hand, are to remain constant.

The managing director, however, has focused only on the positive aspects of his expansion policy: the increased turnover and corresponding increase in cash flowing into the business. What he has not taken into account is the additional cash outflow that will be required to finance the expansion before the increased level of turnover is actually achieved. If, for example, new or additional overdraft facilities are required, the company's bankers need to be informed to ensure that the bank will agree to the facility. In order to achieve this, the potential requirement needs to be quantified, which can only be done by preparing a projected profit and loss account and cashflow, to provide some basis for discussion. Even if it believed that the company can support the additional activity without outside financial support, this assumption needs to be 'proved' by the same means.

The same principles would apply if the company planned

to diversify into the area of supplying, say, garden sheds. Assuming that these are bought in ready-made from a manufacturer, the company needs to assess its required stock-holding levels, whether there is a need for further employees to sell the sheds to new and existing customers, whether additional storage space is required and so on. Although it might be believed that the diversification is a natural progression from the company's existing activities, the effect on the company's financial position must be assessed.

Business goals may be very simple ones, such as aiming to reduce bank overdraft facilities by 50 per cent over the course of a financial year. While it may seem possible to achieve this goal by cutting back on expenditure, it is very difficult to assess exactly how expenditure can be cut back without quantifying existing expenses and determining which can be reduced. Again, a good starting point is the previous year's accounts – assuming that these have been prepared reasonably soon after the business's year-end. Even if it is not immediately obvious where economies might be achieved, the exercise is a useful one for focusing attention on business performance, both past and future.

Ideally, smaller businesses should prepare projections on an annual basis, incorporating realistic expectations for existing activities and any plans for changes in the business. In the same way that good accounting records can help to highlight potential problems in a business, financial projections should help to alert the business owner or manager to difficulties which might arise in the short-term future, and thereby allow time for remedial action to be taken.

## Using financial projections to set budgets

Once projections have been prepared, they should be used to benefit the business. They will be of no use if they are filed away and forgotten until it is time to repeat the exercise next year.

A projected profit and loss account can be used on a regular basis to monitor 'actual' business performance, and this is discussed in more detail in chapter 5. By monitoring expected against actual performance, any significant variances will be highlighted at an early stage. The reasons for material variances can be examined and acted upon, either by amending plans which have proved unrealistic or by reassessing aspects of the business itself.

Similarly, actual cashflow can be compared with projected cashflow. The process works in two ways, as with the profit and loss account. If bank balances prove to be substantially less than those projected, the reasons can be investigated. Was the cashflow projection unrealistic? Are debtors paying more slowly than they used to? Are creditors becoming more stringent in demanding prompt payment? Have overhead expenses increased unexpectedly. . . ?

It is only by focusing attention on these matters that a business can maintain the best possible degree of control over its performance. Of course, if a major customer is lost, for example, there may be little that the business can do to remedy the situation in the short term. However, it will have a far better idea of the impact of such an event on overall business performance than if no projections have been prepared.

A two-partner advertizing agency coped extremely well with exactly this problem. The business had been established for some five years, and had built up a portfolio of both large and small clients. The standard of financial control and planning was generally good, with the exception of the recharge to clients of indirect expenses incurred on their behalf. When a client which represented 10 per cent of turnover was lost to a competitor, the worried partners reworked their projected results for the year ahead. They came to the conclusion that gross profit margins could be significantly improved if a greater effort was made to recharge all expenses incurred on behalf of clients. This would mitigate against the effects of the drop in turnover.

Their efforts were proven in the agency's year-end results. Turnover had indeed dropped by some 10 per cent, but the gross profit margin had increased from 33 per cent to 41 per cent. Overheads had been closely controlled, and were at the same level as the previous year. The overall result was an increase in net profits of over 20 per cent.

In short, the concern caused by the loss of a client and the resulting improvement in cost control had resulted in an increase in profits for the partnership. Clearly, this will not be achieveable for every business, but it serves to illustrate how even a well-controlled business can find areas where this control can be improved.

## Financial projections for external use

Any business which wants to raise finance from external sources such as a bank will be required to prepare cash and profit projections to support its case. For a new business, a clear and concise outline will also be required describing:

- the business activity;
- the market;
- strengths, weaknesses, opportunities and threats;
- short- and longer-term aims, including how these are to be achieved;
- the people running the business;
- required finance
- projected financial position, based on the projections.

For an existing business, a short history of the business will also be required, which includes a summary of recent performance, backed up by accounts.

It is a good idea, especially if the business owner or manager is inexperienced in preparing financial projections, to ask an adviser or a more experienced and trusted associate to look at the projections before presenting them to a bank or other external party.

In periods of difficult economic conditions, raising finance can be extremely difficult: some clearing banks cease to offer finance to new businesses altogether. This should not be regarded as a reason for overstating the business's case, either in words or figures, in an attempt to convince a potential lender that the business is or will be a stable and profitable one when this is not the case. The presentation of misleading projections is unlikely to benefit any of the parties involved. Experienced lenders are able to see through unrealistic plans, and from the business owner's point of view self-deception as to the future success of the business will ultimately be of no constructive use at all.

## Raising finance

Raising and maintaining appropriate levels of finance are necessary for any business, so that adequate funds are available to support both trading operations and capital expenditure. For the smaller business, there are various sources of finance, and the type sought will depend largely on the business itself, and on the purpose for which it is required. It would not be appropriate, for example, to attempt to finance the purchase of premises with a bank overdraft or, conversely, to purchase a car with a ten-year loan if the car is likely to be replaced after three years.

Businesses often fail because they have inadequate working capital with which to support their day-to-day activities, and financing requirements should be considered in conjunction with short- and medium-term financial projections.

## Short-term finance

### Bank overdraft

The bank overdraft is the most common source of finance for smaller companies. Up to a pre-arranged limit, the business borrows only the amount required on a day-to-day basis, rather than having a commitment to a fixed sum which may at various times exceed or fall short of the business's requirements. It is the easiest form of finance to arrange, and interest is paid only on the basis of the amount outstanding each day. Interest will usually be in the range of 2 to 5 per cent over base rate, depending on the bank's assessment of the business and the risk to which it is exposed. Additionally, an annual charge will be levied for arranging or renewing the overdraft, generally up to 1 per cent of the overdraft facility.

An overdraft is most suitable for providing working capital to support the normal trading operations of the business, particularly in its early years. Security will be required by the bank, often in the form of a charge over the assets of the business and also a personal guarantee by the borrower, which is supported by a charge over personal assets such as property. While personal guarantees are generally to be avoided as far as possible, it is extremely unlikely that any bank will be prepared to offer an overdraft facility without such a guarantee, particularly when economic conditions are poor. Indeed, there are increasing numbers of cases where banks are simply not prepared to offer overdraft facilities to new businesses at all.

> One such case concerns a new business in pig farming. A realistic business plan had been drawn up, which indicated that a facility of £20,000 was required to finance the start-up, and that the business should begin to generate a significant positive cash flow by the middle of year two. Substantial security in the form of a charge over personal property and a personal guarantee by a second individual, which was backed by substantial personal assets, were offered. Several clearing banks were approached, and all rejected the proposal, in spite of the security offered.

Businesses should also beware that banks are entitled to the repayment of overdrafts on demand, and that this does occur, especially where the facility has been abused. This is an increasingly common cause of business failure, and should not be treated lightly.

## Longer-term finance

### Term loans

Term loans are generally used for the purchase of equipment or other specific items of capital expenditure, rather than to provide additional working capital for the overall operation of a business. Loans are available from various sources, although for smaller businesses, the most usual is a bank.

Again, security will be required, and there will also be an arrangement fee. A loan is repayable over an agreed number of years, with interest charges usually in the range of 3 to 6 per cent over bank base rate. The rate may either be fixed or floating, the latter being dependent on base rates.

In normal circumstances, one of the advantages of a term loan is that it will not be repayable on demand to the bank, as an overdraft is. However, it is important to be clear about the circumstances in which a bank might demand repayment. These will be contained within the small print of the loan agreement, which *must* be read carefully prior to signature and *not* signed blindly in the belief that the terms of the agreement are standard. Such circumstances might include default in repayments of the loan, or if the value of the security given to the bank falls below the amount of the outstanding loan, as can occur in times of recession.

As with bank overdrafts, banks have become increasingly reluctant to offer new or increased loan facilities to businesses, and in particular, start-ups, regardless of how healthy the business might be.

## Factoring and sales invoice discounting

Factoring and sales invoice discounting are described in detail in chapter 5, and can make a significant difference to a business's cashflow: the difference between receiving cash representing 80 per cent of the value of invoices from a factor in 30 days rather than 100 per cent from a debtor in, say, 90 days is likely to impact substantially on bank balances. Although factoring interest and charges will be levied, these may well may not be great compared with the overdraft interest which might otherwise have been suffered. Equally importantly, the use of a factor can release valuable time otherwise spent chasing debtors.

It is likely that a factor will not be prepared to accept all of a business's sales invoices for factoring, and will carry out their own checks on a business's customers before deciding which it will accept. Another important issue that should be considered is the potential cash deficit which will occur when a business stops factoring its debts. To avoid the requirement for bank overdraft facilities, the business needs to build up a substantial cash reserve to cover the period until debtors pay. There may be a period of one or two months between ceasing to receive cash from the factor and beginning to receive cash direct from debtors again.

It may also be necessary to obtain the agreement of the business's bankers to the use of a factor, if the bank has a charge over the business's assets. Clearly, debtors represent a part of those assets, and, in many businesses, a significant part. For this reason some banks may not give their agreement.

It should be pointed out that although factoring has become far more accepted in recent years, factoring houses are fairly particular about the clients they accept. These are most likely to be stable, well-managed and profitable growing companies, with an annual turnover in excess of £200,000, although new businesses will also be considered.

The Association of British Factors and Discounters in London can provide details of the larger financial and banking groups which provide factoring services. In recent years, there has also been an increase in smaller financial services companies which include factoring services.

## Equity finance

The above tend to be the more common sources of finance for smaller businesses. A further source which is available to limited liability companies only is equity finance. Additional shares can be issued to external parties who are not connected with the business. Many owners of smaller businesses are extremely reluctant to consider equity finance, as they fear a loss of control over a business which they have nurtured and built up over a number of years. However, this may be outweighed by the benefits of a source of finance which is cheaper than bank borrowing, and possibly the business skills of the investor if a representative of the investing body joins the company's board as a non-executive director.

Finding and approaching appropriate potential investors can present a problem: accountants, stockbrokers and local enterprise agencies may be able to help. There are many sources of risk capital, ranging from the clearing banks, merchant banks, 3i and numerous other financial institutions. Stoy Hayward produce a useful guide to sources of venture capital, *Venture Capital 1992*, which includes a number of institutions offering relatively small amounts of capital to smaller and younger businesses, and which should be obtainable free of charge.

While financial projections are often only prepared by smaller businesses in conjunction with an application for additional finance, the exercise should not be regarded as a necessary evil. The benefit to the business may not seem immediately obvious compared with, say, a marketing campaign to increase the customer base. However, it is really the only means to quantify expected future business performance, and to determine whether that marketing campaign is really necessary.

# 5. Accounting issues

The importance of effective accounting control in any business cannot be over-emphasized. A structured and controlled accounting system will not prevent a business from failing, but it will provide the information necessary for managers and owners to make informed decisions and to keep abreast of business performance.

In a small or medium-sized business, the accounting and finance function often comprises a book-keeper and the business manager, with periodic assistance from an external firm of accountants. The fact that the business does not have a larger and dedicated finance team is no reason why a formal accounting system, however simple, should not be operated. Although often regarded as a time-consuming administrative nuisance, the maintenance of basic accounting books and records will undoubtedly benefit the vast majority of businesses.

An issue which commonly emerges when a business is facing failure is a lack of awareness of the scale of its financial difficulties. In many cases, these could have been reduced by an improved knowledge of the financial position of the business and positive action to strengthen it, or at least to mitigate the effects.

This does not mean that accounting information is of greater importance *per se* when a business is suffering as a result of, say, poor economic conditions. The immediate needs of the business might change in their emphasis so that, for example, much tighter control is exercised over debtors and bank balances. However, these issues are no less important when the business appears to be achieving good results: how else can the business owner or manager actually make accurate judgements of how good those results and their various constituent elements are?

It is vital to ensure not only that accounting information is available to comply with, for example, limited company legislation and VAT accounting requirements, but also that it is tailored to be appropriate to the needs of the business, and that it is acted upon. While the accounting requirements of businesses will vary in terms of information content, they will share common aims, which can be grouped broadly under four headings:

- Product costing
- Budgetary control
- Cashflow planning
- Working capital management.

It may seem at times that advisers such as accountants or bank managers are excessively concerned with these matters, while the business owner or manager is already over-taxed coping with the day-to-day problems of running a business. However, time spent on maintaining accounting systems can bring enormous benefits by providing accurate and up-to-date information which will help both decision-making and the financial control of the business.

## Product costing

The process of determining an appropriate selling price for a product or service is one which needs to be reviewed on a regular basis. A deterioration in levels of profitability can quickly result from setting a price either too high or too low – or indeed relying on an *ad hoc* pricing policy.

The basic aims when determining a selling price for a product or service can be summarized as:

- to be competitive;
- to cover all costs incurred and to make a profit.

These aims cannot be achieved by guesswork, and some product costing methods are described in chapter 4.

In periods of poor economic conditions, it may prove difficult to achieve these aims. If, for example, competitors reduce their selling prices to stimulate demand, it is important not to respond to such problems by slashing selling prices in a panic reaction. It is equally important not to ignore such a problem by assuming that customer loyalty will override the temptation of cheaper prices elsewhere.

Clearly, certain cases will arise where it is necessary to offer customer discounts, particularly if a customer is a long-standing one. However, there is a fine balance between retaining custom and reducing prices to such a degree that the business no longer covers its costs. It is therefore necessary to know to what degree a business can suffer a decline in selling prices before it ceases to cover its costs and make a reasonable profit. This forms part of the price-setting and planning process, but it should also be remembered that trading conditions and business circumstances do change, and pricing policy should be subject to review on a regular basis.

For example, a business sells an average of 1,000 units per month at a selling price of £50 per unit. The direct cost per unit is an average of £35, and overhead costs are in the region of £12,500 per month. If the selling price is reduced to £45 per unit, but the number of units sold and the cost per unit remain constant, the price cut will have the following effect on the business's profit and loss account:

|  | Selling price £50 | Selling price £45 |
| --- | --- | --- |
| Sales | 50,000 | 45,000 |
| Direct costs | 35,000 | 35,000 |
| Gross profit | 15,000 | 10,000 |
| | | |
| Overheads | 12,500 | 12,500 |
| Net profit / (loss) | | |
| before tax and interest | £ 2,500 | £(2,500) |

The example is a simplistic one, but illustrates the effect of reducing selling prices simply to maintain demand, without thinking through the implications to their conclusion. There will also be an adverse affect on the business's bank balance, as cash inflows are reduced, which may well lead to an increase in bank interest charges, thus eroding the net profit even further.

This problem can be mitigated against – up to a point – by taking positive steps to promote customer loyalty. In the case of product sales, this might take the form of emphasizing quality, of providing test samples of new products or of setting and attaining high standards of reliability. For example, if a business offers a 24-hour delivery service and consistently manages to achieve this goal, customers are likely – consciously or otherwise – to regard the business favourably, whether its product is better than that offered by competitors or not. Conversely, a business which sells a widely available range of products such as stationery supplies, but which is frequently out of stock of required items, or which takes weeks to deliver the goods, is unlikely to succeed in building up a core of satisfied and loyal customers.

Where a business is offering a service, loyalty is likely to be generated by combining efficiency and professionalism with a 'tender, loving care' approach to customer or client relations: the latter factor has a more significant effect on achieving 'repeat business' than is often appreciated. A business which (from the customer's perception) treats customers in an offhand manner is potentially throwing away the opportunity of further business, both from that customer and via the grapevine. Owners and managers of small businesses do consult each other as to the quality of services received from, for example, solicitors, accountants, printers and insurance brokers, and word of mouth can be a valuable source of business.

## Budgetary control

Budgetary control refers to the process of monitoring actual against expected income and costs, both direct and indirect. The purpose of budgetary control is to ensure that any significant differences between expected events and actual trading activities can be acted upon swiftly. These differences may be positive, such as higher than expected sales, or negative, such as spiralling costs.

The exercise of effective budgetary control assumes that an adequate budget or projected profit and loss account has been prepared, and this process is covered in chapter 4.

One of the purposes of preparing a budget is to provide a yardstick against which actual business performance can be measured. Except perhaps in the start-up period, the majority of businesses have a reasonably informed idea of the level of sales they are expecting for a given period, and the direct and indirect costs they will incur against these sales. During the first year of trading as well, business owners and managers should take steps to ensure that likely levels of costs have been adequately re-searched.

Ideally, budgets should be monitored on a regular, say, monthly or quarterly basis, and in conjunction with management accounts. In this way, any significant departure from expected results can be acted upon swiftly. If, for example, direct costs have increased as a result of price increases by suppliers but selling prices have remained static, it follows that gross profit margins will be eroded. If the level of erosion is such that gross profits are no longer sufficient to cover indirect costs – i.e. the running costs of the business such as rent, telephone and administration salaries – plans for the short-term future will require revision. This might take various forms.

It might be decided to implement an increase in selling prices, if it is felt that customer loyalty can still be preserved. Conversely, alternative suppliers might be found who can offer goods or services at lower prices. In both cases, the aim is to return the business to a healthy level of gross profitability. In conjunction with this, it may prove possible to achieve savings in running costs. By comparing budgeted with actual levels of running costs, it should be possible to identify those areas where diver-gences exist, and to determine whether certain categories of cost can be reduced.

An example of an actual compared with a budgeted profit and loss account is set out below.

In this case, there are a number of areas which might warrant investigation. Sales are lower than the budgeted level, but of more concern, the gross profit margin shows a fairly significant variance. Did this result from reductions in selling prices, increased costs from suppliers, a need to buy in emergency stocks at higher prices, inefficiency – or was the budget unrealistic? How does the margin compare with prior periods' results?

Similarly, although certain categories of overhead fall below the budgeted level, others are well in excess, and some did not

| | Quarter Actual | Quarter Budget |
|---|---:|---:|
| Sales | 90,109 | 110,000 |
| Cost of sales | 66,023 | 73,333 |
| Gross profit | **24,086** | **36,667** |
| Gross profit % | **26.73%** | **33.33%** |
| | | |
| Transport costs | 6,004 | 4,800 |
| Wages and salaries | 7,775 | 7,775 |
| Motor vehicle expenses | 644 | 1,000 |
| Travel expenses | 737 | 600 |
| Hotel & subsistence | 657 | 500 |
| Entertaining | 200 | 250 |
| Advertising | 7,215 | 5,000 |
| Printing, postage & stationery | 525 | 1,000 |
| Training | – | 550 |
| Operating leases | 169 | 192 |
| Telephone | 2,460 | 1,500 |
| Insurance | 1,727 | 2,000 |
| Rates & service charge | 1,043 | 1,100 |
| Electricity | 80 | 100 |
| Accountancy | 400 | 400 |
| Secretarial services | 250 | – |
| Sundry expenses | 172 | 300 |
| Repairs and renewals | 117 | – |
| Depreciation | 2,616 | 2,500 |
| Bank charges | 462 | 350 |
| Bank interest | 315 | 250 |
| Hire purchase interest | 473 | – |
| | 34,041 | 30,167 |
| Net (loss) / profit | **£(9,955)** | **£ 6,500** |

figure at all in the budget. While there is no point in investigating minor, one-off cost overruns (the time taken will probably outweigh any potential cost saving), larger discrepancies or unexpected costs do merit examination, so that a greater degree of control can be exercised in the future, if necessary.

Although it is clear that this is a business which makes considerable effort to prepare accurate budgets, the cost categories which might be looked at in more detail include transport, advertising and telephone costs.

There are no set rules determining where cost savings can be made. However, business owners and managers should, by the process of monitoring budgets, be in a position to identify at the earliest possible opportunity those areas where costs need more careful control, or, indeed, where budgets were unrealistic and require modification.

The process of preparing formal budgets or trading projections is one to which many businesses devote little time, although most business owners and managers may have a fair idea of their expectations of sales and associated costs, even if these are not formalized. If, for example, sales are high value and low volume, it may be difficult to predict accurately more than a few months in advance what the level of turnover is expected to be. However, the indirect running costs of the business are unlikely to fluctuate to the same degree, and a manager might know from experience of prior periods' trading that these should be in the region of, say, £5,000 per month. It may be in such a case that in some isolated months this level of costs is not adequately covered by gross profits, but that over a period of, say, six months, the business will generate sufficient gross profit to cover its costs. If costs were to increase significantly to £10,000 per month, as a result of a rent review coupled with the employment of additional staff, for example, it would be vital for the business manager to ensure, based on prior periods' results and expectations of future trading, that the business is still able to cover its costs.

The business which does not prepare any form of budget or management accounts on a regular basis is the one which is likely to suffer most deeply and quickly when trading problems begin to arise. Because there exists no yardstick against which to measure performance, problems such as the over-run of costs, whether direct in the form of materials or direct labour, or indirect in the form of administrative expenses, are not identified as they arise and may persist for some months before they become evident. It may be a lack of cash resources which first alerts a business manager to such problems, where it emerges that costs have been gradually increasing, whereas turnover has remained static. While a sudden cost increase may be noticed promptly, the impact of apparently small increases in a number of cost categories may not be realized until it becomes obvious that a serious cash shortage exists.

In almost every case, some mitigating action can be taken if problems are recognized sufficiently early. This may take the form of a decision to cease trading, if it is felt that the business can not reasonably be expected to return to a satisfactory level of profitability. This may appear an unnecessarily negative view, but an early decision can make the difference between the relatively straightforward liquidation of a business and personal ruin.

Budget monitoring does not need to be the time-consuming and complicated exercise which it may at first appear. The essential point is to become aware of unexpected or unforeseen events, however minor they might seem, and to take appropriate action as soon as possible. This may involve modifications to the business or indeed modifications to the budget. There is no point at all in spending both time and money on the preparation of budgets or projections if they are not subsequently used for the benefit of the business. Even if they are later proved to be 'wrong', they have at least provided a means of focusing attention upon short-term business activities.

## Cashflow planning

Cashflow planning is an integral part of the operation of any business, whether the process is formal and documented in consultation with financial advisers or carried out on an informal, 'What can we afford?' basis. In the latter case, the process can easily begin to take on the somewhat precarious form of a juggling exercise, which can often result in near-disaster.

Effective cashflow planning can make the difference between the survival and failure of a business. Cashflow planning – as distinct from working capital management, which is discussed below – is therefore essential. An example of cashflow forecast is set out in chapter 4.

In this context, cashflow planning refers to the broader aspects of cash management, rather than immediate, day-to-day issues such as whether to pay certain creditors or chase certain debtors, which are discussed in 'Working capital management' below.

It is necessary to reach decisions regarding the business's policy for, among other things,

- the payment of creditors;
- terms of credit offered to customers;
- the level of capital expenditure the business requires and can bear.

Obviously, terms for the payment of creditors will depend largely on what is dictated by suppliers of goods and services, HM Customs and Excise and the Inland Revenue, amongst others. However, regardless of credit terms, payments can be made only if sufficient cash (or indeed overdraft facility) is available. Terms of credit offered to customers must therefore not be so generous as to lead to a shortfall in available cash for the payment of creditors.

Although it might be tempting to offer incentives to customers in the form of, say, 90 days credit, this will not benefit the business in the long term – or indeed the short term – if cash runs out and suppliers withdraw credit because of late payment of invoices. If such incentives are to be considered, a careful and detailed cashflow forecast covering at least a twelve-month period should be drawn up first to assess the impact on the business's bank account.

Capital expenditure requirements will vary from business to business depending upon the nature of their trading activities. Businesses operating in service sectors will probably have a relatively low level of fixed assets, mainly office equipment and motor vehicles. This will differ greatly from the business involved in a manufacturing process, which will also require plant and machinery to manufacture its products.

In periods of recession there is often a conflict between the desire to present an impression of a successful business, by operating from smart, expensively furnished premises and re-newing motor vehicles relatively frequently, and pressures on cashflow which dictate that, say, the renewal of cars will put unnecessary strain on cash resources.

> An independent financial adviser who sold insurance policies did not see the pressure that this type of expenditure was putting on his business. Although the business was still in its infancy, this adviser believed it was important to present an impressive image by means of an expensive car funded by a bank loan and rented premises, when he could easily have worked from home. As he quickly discovered, the business was simply unable to support this level of expenditure.
>
> The business was wound up after less than two years' trading, with a level of debt which forced the sale of his home. The situation could have been avoided had he taken a more realistic view of his trading prospects.

Alternatives to the outright purchase of fixed assets include leasing and hire purchase, which spread the cash outflow over a longer period. Operating leases differ from finance leases and hire purchase in that in the former case, ownership of the asset remains with the lessor – the business or lessee does not gain ownership of the asset at the end of the period of the lease. It has the advantage that a business can acquire the use of an asset without having to suffer the entire cost immediately. In a market where technology is continuously advancing, the company may also wish to enjoy the advantage of replacing, say, its computers every three or four years without having to suffer the major capital outlay involved each time.

Hire purchase and finance leasing is probably used by busi-nesses most frequently for the acquisition of motor vehicles. For example, a business acquires a new car for which the cash price is £10,090, and pays a deposit of £5,000. The monthly repayments, if phased over two years, are calculated as follows:

| | |
|---|---:|
| Cash price | 10,090.00 |
| Less : deposit | 5,000.00 |
| Balance | 5,090.00 |
| Interest charge (APR 20.1%) | 992.56 |
| Administration & option charge | 40.00 |
| Total payable | **£6,122.56** |
| | |
| Monthly repayments | |
| Month 1 | 283.44 |
| Months 2–23 @ 253.44 | 5,575.68 |
| Month 24 | 263.44 |
| Total | **£6,122.56** |

It should be noted that it is only when the option charge is paid (this is included in the final repayment) that ownership of the car is transferred to the business.

Alternatively, a much smaller deposit may be paid (often three months' worth of repayments) with repayments phased over three years. For example, a van is purchased by a small business as follows:

| | |
|---|---:|
| Cash price | 9,380.93 |
| Less : deposit (including 3 months' repayments) | 2,244.95 |
| Balance | 7,135.98 |
| Interest charge (APR 11.5%) | 1,159.89 |
| Total payable | **£8,295.87** |
| | |
| Monthly repayments | |
| 33 × 251.39 | **£8,295.87** |

Although the interest rate in the second example is considerably lower, the actual interest charge is higher because the credit period is longer. However, it may still be less than the interest charge for a bank loan, for example. The only way to determine this is to investigate the credit terms offered on vehicles with garages or leasing companies and to discuss loan terms with banks – if they are prepared to offer a loan – to determine which is the preferable source of finance.

According to UK Accounting Standards, assets held under

finance leases have to be capitalized in the business's balance sheet. This means that the leased asset is included in fixed assets in the balance sheet, and the corresponding liability to the leasing company is included in creditors, split as appropriate between liabilities due within one year and due after more than one year. In contrast, assets leased under operating leases are not capitalized, but the 'rentals' payable are charged direct to the profit and loss account in the period to which they relate.

The distinction may not appear immediately significant, but it does make a difference to the business's current balance sheet position, and also to its asset turnover ratios. Because no liability is included in the balance sheet, operating leases can provide a form of off-balance sheet financing. Although the business may have to meet the lease payments for a number of years, no borrowings are indicated in the balance sheet, and the business may appear to be in a stronger borrowing position than one which has opted for a finance lease. The impact of a finance lease on the balance sheet total, however, will be nil, because the liability to the leasing company will be offset by the cost included in fixed assets.

The sale and leaseback of fixed assets can be considered to generate immediate cash from assets which are already owned by the business. This strategy is more commonly used in conjunction with property, where a business owns the freehold or it is held under a long lease, and with plant and machinery. Sale and leaseback has the advantage that the business still retains the use of the asset, while securing a cash inflow for the business which can be used for other purposes.

For example, a business might sell its freehold property to a finance company, and then make rental payments to the finance company for the use of the property. Obviously, there are potential drawbacks to such a transaction. Although the business still has the use of the property (or other asset), it no longer owns it. Eventually the period of the lease will end, and the business may have to find alternative assets. In the case of property, the business must also forego the potential capital appreciation. These drawbacks may be considered to be costs of the transaction, in addition to the rental payments made.

The advantage of the immediate availability of a relatively large sum of cash which can be used to the benefit of the business will often outweigh the potential loss to the business of the ownership of its property. However, the decision is not one which can be generalized, and should be considered carefully by any business considering this strategy.

## Working capital management

Working capital management, if carried out efficiently, can vastly improve the financial stability of a business, particularly in the short term. The effective management of stocks, debtors and creditors can have a significant positive impact on a business's cash position, which can ultimately make the difference between survival and failure. Many businesses fail because poor management leads to a lack of working capital with which to support the business.

Business managers can make a very positive contribution to the management of:

- bank account
- debtors
- stocks
- creditors.

### Bank account

The theory put forward by Keynes to explain motives for holding cash states, in summary, that in ideal conditions a business holds sufficient cash to cover transactions, precautionary balances and speculative balances.

The *transactions motive* refers to the cash required to cover the normal trading operations of the business. Given that cash inflows are more difficult to control than outflows, there will often be a time lag between incurring and paying for the costs associated with a sale and receiving payment for it. A cash balance is therefore required to cover this temporary shortfall.

The *precautionary motive* refers to cash held for reasons of caution in case of unexpected liabilities. It is generally not possible to forecast cash requirements with absolute accuracy, and ideally, the more uncertain are predictions of future cashflow, the greater the precautionary cash balance needs to be.

The *speculation motive* refers to a requirement to hold cash to cover immediately any profitable business transactions which may arise unexpectedly. This will apply most commonly to the business whose normal trading activities are largely speculative.

In practice, and particularly in difficult economic conditions, the majority of small and medium businesses are simply not in a position to maintain cash balances in excess of their immediate needs, and many may be dependent on bank overdraft facilities to cover even these.

The use of overdrafts by small businesses is extremely common, since the overdraft facility offers a simple and flexible source of short-term finance. It enjoys the advantage over a term loan that the business borrows – and pays interest on – only the amount it requires immediately, rather than a pre-arranged fixed sum. Banks do, however, expect overdraft balances to fluctuate, and if an account is permanently operated close to its overdraft limit, a bank may seek to convert part or all of the balance to a loan account. This need not necessarily be a disadvantage, but may be a sign that the bank is concerned for the security of its lendings.

Dealings with bankers are discussed in more detail below.

Although bank balances are also dependent upon the management of debtors, creditors and so on, control over bank accounts can be improved by implementing simple procedures.

If the business generates a high volume of transactions, the bank balance should be checked daily, or at least weekly, taking into account cheques which have been written and amounts paid into the account which do not yet appear on the most recent bank statement. This is a procedure which should be carried out formally in any case on a monthly basis, so that the business manager never loses track of cash availability or likely shortfalls.

In a small or medium business, the authorization and signature of cheques should ideally be carried out by one individual. The business which allows a number of individuals to write cheques with no central control over their combined effect on the bank account will quickly lose control over its bank balance.

It is also sensible to transfer any surplus cash in a current account to an interest-bearing account, to gain some benefit from a positive cash position. Some banks will arrange for a constant balance to be maintained in a current account by means of transfers to and from an interest-bearing account. If the balance envisaged to be held in an interest-bearing account is relatively small, however, take care that bank charges for providing the service do not outweigh the benefit of the interest earned. Policy for offering this service varies from bank to bank (some have ceased to provide it altogether), and terms should be carefully checked and agreed in writing.

These points may seem obvious, and indeed they are largely based on common sense. However, it is often the simple procedures which focus attention on an issue and lead to an improved level of management.

## Debtors

The effective management of debtors can become problematic in periods of economic downturn, when customers understandably tend to stretch credit terms to their limit. Efforts can be made to speed up cash inflows by various means.

First, sales invoices should be raised and sent out to customers promptly. It may seem more efficient to raise batches of invoices, say, once a month, but this can effectively result in providing customers with additional weeks of free credit.

Prompt settlement discounts can be offered as an incentive to customers if they pay within a specified time limit. The benefit of receiving payment promptly must be weighed up against the loss to the business of the value of the discount. There is some doubt as to the effectiveness of prompt settlement discounts, and there exists an additional danger that the discount is taken by the customer regardless of when the invoice is paid. If the monetary value of the discount is small, the time taken to recover it later might well be disproportionately great.

The right to charge interest on amounts which are not paid by their due dates can be included in 'Terms and Conditions' of sale on the face of sales invoices. This can help to persuade customers not to exceed credit terms, particularly where sales invoices are of high value.

Non-refundable deposits can be charged before the commencement of work or the supply of a product. This will be most relevant where the work carried out by the business will span a relatively long period of time, such that the business will incur costs itself well before the completion of the work. A deposit representing a proportion of the estimated final cost of the work can be requested by the business as a form of insurance against the recovery of its costs.

Effective credit control is essential. It is very easy, particularly where sales are of low value and high volume, to allow the business's level of debtors to creep up to an unhealthy level. Small invoices may not appear to be worth the effort of chasing, but these can quickly mount up in total value and the business's cash position can deteriorate as a result. Where a large volume of sales invoices is generated, it becomes more difficult to keep track of outstanding amounts. The importance of maintaining accounting records whereby debtors can be monitored increases. If it is not possible to maintain individual debtor's accounts, then a Sales Day Book which records sales invoice details, including payment dates, will facilitate monitoring of overdue amounts.

In periods of poor economic conditions, even the most strenuous efforts at credit control can prove only partially successful. It may be that customers themselves are suffering from serious cash problems, and are simply unable to pay invoices as they fall due. Running credit checks and requesting credit references before providing a new customer with credit facilities can help to reduce this problem.

Factoring sales ledger debts can provide a means of improving a business's level of working capital. Rightly or wrongly, the perception of a business which factors its debts has in the past been largely negative. However, that perception has changed in recent years, and for some businesses factoring may be a sensible option where there is a need to speed up cash inflows, perhaps to fund an increased level of turnover.

There are three main types of factoring, which will provide up to around 80 per cent of the value of outstanding invoices. The factoring company will make a service charge based on the level of turnover, usually in the range of 0.1 per cent to 2.5 per cent and a finance charge, usually in the order of 2.5 to 4 per cent over base rate.

Full service factoring offers a complete sales ledger management service. The business is responsible simply for raising sales invoices and credit notes. These are recorded by the factor, who also sends out debtors' statements, receives cash as it falls due and chases overdue amounts, arranging legal proceedings to recover debts where necessary. In addition, credit cover can be arranged, whereby the factor assesses a potential customer's creditworthiness and provides insurance for approved customers up to an agreed limit against any bad debts. Usually, up to 80 per cent of the value of the invoices is advanced to the business, based on a calculated average settlement date.

The service charge costs for full service factoring are higher than for other forms of factoring, and are calculated to cover administration costs, taking into account the number of customer accounts open, the number of invoices raised, customer credit risk and so on.

If a factor is managing a business's sales ledger customers will be aware that the business is using a factor to speed up its cash flows. This used to be regarded as a serious disadvantage but factoring is now more widely seen as a valid source of credit alongside bank overdraft and trade credit facilities.

Bulk factoring, or sales finance factoring, differs from full service factoring in that the business continues to manage its own sales ledger. Up to around 80 per cent of the value of sales invoices is provided by the factor immediately, but the business remains responsible for collecting the debts and paying them into the factor's own bank account. This service is available with or without credit protection cover, and is cheaper than full service financing. The balance of the debt is usually remitted, less charges, when the debt has been recovered in full by the factor.

Invoice discounting provides finance based on up to 80 per cent of outstanding debtor balances rather than on specific invoices.

As with bulk factoring, the business remains responsible for collecting debts and paying them into the factor's bank account. The service charge tends to be lower than for other forms of factoring, although the finance charge can be higher.

Although factoring and invoice discounting are suitable for most types of manufacturing, distribution and service businesses, a factoring house will try to satisfy itself that the business is a suitable candidate for its services. It will not regard as suitable a business which is suffering declining gross profit margins or turnover, or one which plans to fund fixed asset purchases from the initial cash inflow from the factor.

From the viewpoint of the factoring house, funds advanced from factoring should be used to finance current and not long term operations. The ideal candidate, perhaps, is the successful and stable small or medium business which has a fast-growing order book but does not have the working capital to finance the growth (to fund increased orders from suppliers, for example). Speeding up cash inflows from debtors can avoid the necessity of turning to increased bank borrowing to fund growth.

It should be remembered, however, that although remittances from debtors will generally be received sooner than they would otherwise have been, the benefit of an increase in cash inflows is a one-off event. The cost of the service is also a major issue. The benefit to the business of an improvement in short-term liquidity and perhaps a reduction in bank overdraft interest payable must be weighed up against the charges levied by the factoring house.

## Stocks

Stocks may be divided into three categories:

- raw materials
- work in progress
- finished goods.

Each category requires control and management to achieve the optimum stock-holding, which will be dependent on anticipated levels of sales and of production, and on the time lags which arise on delivery to customers and ordering from suppliers. The safety factor must also be taken into account, whereby a buffer of stocks may be held to guard against an unexpected upturn in sales, or a supplier's failure to deliver on time.

Certain costs may increase in direct proportion to the level of stocks held, such as storage and transport charges, as well as the potential costs of obsolescence in certain markets and the 'opportunity cost' of tying up cash in stocks. However, these must be compared with the possible benefits of achieving bulk discounts from suppliers for purchasing larger quantities of goods on a less frequent basis, and reducing the danger of stock shortages which might hold up the production process.

The exercise of effective stock control will depend up to a point on the type of products or materials held by the business: one which sells stationery supplies will have certain requirements which differ from a business which manufactures and sells computer hardware.

A formal system of stock control which provides up-to-date information about product lines and numbers of items held may or may not be essential, depending on the type of business. In any case, such a system should be used sensibly, particularly where a business holds hundreds of different items. The administrative cost of maintaining tight control over every single product line may well be out of all proportion to the costs of either overstocking or running out of certain items, particularly where these are of low value and / or can be replaced quickly. Tighter control should be exercised over items where, for instance, there is a relatively long delivery time and where a delay could significantly affect the manufacturing process or result in a loss of custom, or where items have a high individual monetary value. Control should be adopted sensibly in proportion to the overall value of an item.

It is equally sensible to carry out a regular review of stocks, to ensure that excessive cash is not tied up in items which are slow-moving or completely obsolete, especially where these are of high value.

The judgement of 'correct' stockholding levels is not a matter which is subject to hard and fast rules, but is more likely to be achieved by a combination of common sense and experience.

Businesses do make errors of judgement, particularly when it is necessary to forecast sales demand well in advance of the actual sales. However, the business which learns from its mistakes and does not persist in believing that it knows best when a stock line is clearly not selling is the one which will not be left with excessive cash tied up in unsaleable stocks.

## Creditors

### TRADE CREDIT

For the majority of small and medium businesses, trade suppliers represent the largest single source of credit. Without trade credit, it would be necessary for the business to make payment for goods and services well in advance of receiving cash from its customers for the associated sales. The resulting time lag between cash outflows and inflows would potentially lead to a requirement for considerable bank overdraft or loan facilities, which in turn would result in increased interest costs to the business.

Trade credit also has the advantage of relative convenience: to telephone a supplier with an order is much simpler administratively than to send a letter accompanied by a cheque. However, there are few businesses which have not at some time abused the terms of credit offered by suppliers, usually because prompt payment would upset the business's bank position.

There are certain creditors, such as HM Customs and Excise, the Inland Revenue and other statutory bodies, whose payment terms it is extremely unwise to ignore. They have extensive powers to enable them to collect outstanding amounts due to them, and in recent years have become increasingly stringent in applying those powers.

Suppliers of goods and services who remain unpaid for unreasonable periods of time also have resort to legal action to recover amounts due to them, although where the amounts involved are relatively small this can be an expensive and time-consuming option. This does not mean that suppliers will not resort to such means; the result, at worst, can be liquidation or bankruptcy.

Allowing the level of trade creditors to increase in periods of difficult trading conditions is a common reaction by many businesses, in an attempt to limit the deterioration of bank balances. Suppliers chasing overdue payments will often be met with the response that they will receive payment as soon as the business in turn receives anticipated payments from its own customers. If handled with diplomacy, many suppliers are usually willing to accept such reasons, but good communication in these cases is essential. To ignore written requests for payment, or to state in response to a telephone call that 'a cheque is in the post' when it is not, will only have the effect of provoking suppliers and putting future dealings in jeopardy.

If the business is suffering genuine problems of cashflow, then a far more effective approach is an offer of part payment – which will at least demonstrate good faith – and a realistic estimate of the date of full settlement of the invoice. Most creditors will respond more positively to such a proposal than to obvious stalling tactics. Having made a proposal, it is then essential to adhere to it, or to contact the creditor again – before the promised payment date – if there will be difficulties in settlement.

Obviously, if the business continues to default on payments which have been promised to suppliers, then it is to be expected that the supplier's patience will eventually run out. This could result in legal action to recover the outstanding amount and / or in a refusal to supply any further goods or services to the business. Either course of action could have disastrous results for the business.

The key in these cases, then, is good communication. Preempting irate telephone calls or letters can go a long way in preserving good will and maintaining supplies of goods to the business.

These problems tend to be most severe for small businesses, which often have to give more credit to their customers than they receive from their suppliers. They have a disadvantage in terms of their weak bargaining position in relation to the larger businesses which they deal with and may find they have to offer less stringent credit terms to their customers than they would like, whilst having to adhere to the more severe terms dictated by suppliers. Liquidity can be affected quickly and seriously if the effect of credit policies on the business's cash position has been under-estimated.

If a business does not suffer from difficulties in settling invoices from creditors, it must nonetheless formulate a policy for the payment of creditors. Initially, it is necessary to be aware of due dates for invoices, and an adequate recording system for purchase invoices is therefore required. If individual creditor's accounts are not maintained, then a Purchase Day Book in which purchase invoice and payment details are recorded will allow the business to keep track of amounts owed to creditors.

## VALUE ADDED TAX

Most businesses account for VAT on the basis of purchase invoices received and sales invoices issued – the 'accruals' basis. Cash accounting, whereby the VAT is not declared until payment is made or received can be more advantageous for a business which consistently has a higher level of trade debtors than of VAT registered creditors (i.e. outstanding purchase invoices which bear VAT).

This scheme can be applied for only by businesses with a turnover not exceeding £300,000 (in 1992), and if the total amount outstanding to HM Customs and Excise is £5,000 or less (in 1992).

The reason why cash accounting is more advantageous under the circumstances described above is that under the accruals accounting basis, VAT on all of the sales invoices (output VAT) included in trade debtors is declared in the quarter in which they are raised. Under the cash accounting basis, the VAT is not declared until the invoice is paid. Equally, VAT on purchase invoices (input VAT) can not be reclaimed until the invoice is paid, but this apparent disadvantage can be outweighed by the benefit gained from the output VAT.

For the majority of businesses switching from the accruals to the cash accounting basis, there will be a tangible cash benefit in the first quarter of its operation. Thereafter, the benefit will be less apparent, but the business will still gain in cash terms from the 'delayed' declaration of a proportion of its transactions.

Although a business will not gain significantly from such a change, it is one of many factors involved in working capital management which can help the business's liquidity position.

## The role of external advisers

All businesses, whether large or small, need external advisers to provide expert guidance or support at various points throughout the life of the business. For smaller businesses, those with whom they are likely to have most frequent contact are the accountant and the bank manager. Both are often regarded warily, if not with outright suspicion for the benefit of the services they offer. However, if they are chosen with care so that a good working relationship can be established, both parties can make a very positive contribution to the operation and progress of the business.

### Accountants

There exists a widespread mystique around the work carried out by accountants, particularly where contact with the business is limited to an annual visit connected with the preparation or audit of accounts and completion of associated tax returns. This is compounded by the fact that only a relatively small proportion of small business owners and managers acquire or are taught the skill of reading and interpreting the financial statements in any depth. The benefit to the business of the involvement of an external accountant may not therefore be immediately obvious.

Clearly, part of the work of an accountant is to ensure that the business complies with legislation regarding financial statements and taxation. However, the role does not need to be as limited as this, and should be dictated by the requirements of the business. Some businesses do not necessarily require any further assistance on a regular basis.

However, particularly in a still young and growing business which does not have the resources to produce its own management information, the accountant can play an important role. This might, for example, take the form of assistance with maintaining basic accounting books and records, the preparation of periodic management accounts based on records maintained by the business itself, or help with budgeting or the preparation of cash and profit projections.

Of course, all of these exercises result in an increase in accountancy costs, but if properly managed, the improvement in management information and overall control within the business should justify the additional cost. Furthermore, the business itself should benefit from the education process of regular contact with an accountant, which should work in two ways. First, the accountant becomes increasingly familiar with the operations of the business, and is in a better position to identify strengths and weaknesses, and potential opportunities and problems. Second, the business manager's financial management skills should improve, so that dependence on the accountant is gradually decreased.

This all assumes that the working relationship with the accountant is a productive one, and emphasizes the need to choose an individual or firm with which the business feels comfortable. For example, a large international firm of accountants may not be in a position to provide to a small business such an effective hand-holding service as a smaller, local firm which may be more accessible. Alternatively, the smaller firm may not be able to offer dedicated experts for certain types of specialist work. Such considerations should be weighed up and discussed with potentially suitable accountancy firms, which should not make any charge for an initial discussion. The best source of possible firms is probably local business contacts, who can comment from their own experience.

Businesses should also not be afraid to ask accountants to explain clearly any financial issues which they do not fully understand. This might include, for example, guidance on the interpretation of financial statements – and in particular, the balance sheet – or help with modifications to accounting books and records so that improved management information can be produced.

# Bankers

When a business is managing its bank account in accordance with the terms agreed with the bank, it is likely that there will be little contact between the business and its bank manager. In some cases, particularly where loans or overdraft facilities are significant (in terms of the business overall), banks will request regular management accounts, generally quarterly, so that they can monitor their exposure, or the risk they are taking in lending to that business.

Small businesses, and especially young ones, are often at a disadvantage where banks are concerned because they have little or no track record to prove their worth as a good risk for a bank. As a result, they may suffer high interest rates and fees on their bank borrowings – if indeed they succeed in negotiating overdraft or loan facilities. In a recessionary climate where numbers of failing businesses are increasing, banks are in any case reluctant to increase their exposure where there is any likelihood that a business might default or even fail.

It should never be forgotten that bank overdrafts are almost always repayable on demand, and demands from a bank to clear an overdraft have become an increasingly common factor in business failure. Overdrafts are intended to cover short-term cash shortfalls, such as that which often occurs during the business start-up period.

Establishing good communication with a bank manager is essential, particularly when a business manager can foresee cashflow difficulties. Good communication will not necessarily help to save a business which is on the brink of failure. However, as with dealings with trade suppliers, prior notice given to a bank manager of cashflow problems may elicit a more sympathetic response. It is also very much cheaper than suffering charges for letters stating that overdraft limits have been breached, and the embarrassment of bounced cheques written to pay suppliers.

Whether a bank will be open to negotiation regarding overdraft and loan terms will vary from bank to bank. Again, where a business is suffering cashflow difficulties, discussions with the bank to this effect with estimates of significant cash in- and outflows in the immediate future are preferable from the business's viewpoint to the receipt of a letter demanding the repayment of an overdraft in full, or calling in a loan. A bank's response to attempts at the re-negotiation of loan and overdraft facilities will of course vary from bank to bank, and depend on the nature of the relationship between the bank and the business in the past.

Remember above all that a large number of small businesses fail as a result of demands for payment or legal action from bankers and creditors for large, long-outstanding debts.

## Other advisers

From time to time, businesses may need to call on other advisers such as solicitors, pensions advisers or marketing consultants for guidance on business or financial matters. Suitable candidates will obviously vary from business to business depending on their requirements, but again, the grapevine is often a good source, particularly for those advisers who are very good, or those who are to be avoided.

# 6. **Predicting company failure**

The prediction of company failure is an area which tends to attract more scepticism from business owners and managers than from external analysts. This is not surprising: no business owner wants to admit that his or her company is in imminent danger of failing, and it is often difficult to accept such a prediction. In spite of this, techniques which analyse the financial characteristics of a company and provide indications as to the likelihood of failure can supply a useful basis for management decision-making – although they will not be able to supply the cure for failure.

While the emphasis throughout this chapter is on the detection of problem areas in a business, it should not be forgotten that the same techniques can be used to highlight areas in which the business shows greater strengths. Once identified, it should be possible to capitalize upon these to improve both the profitability and stability of the business.

There is always a danger that statistical analysis is presented in such a way that a fairly sophisticated level of financial understanding is required to comprehend its implications fully. This need not be the case, and analysis does not need to be highly technical.

A factor cited as a severe drawback to failure prediction techniques by some sceptics is the 'self-fulfilling prophecy' argument. Somewhat akin to the chicken and egg debate, they argue that failure can in fact be hastened by predictions to that effect, because suppliers of both finance and goods lose confidence in the 'failing' company and withdraw support as a result of negative predictions. These actions may then act as a catalyst for a company failure which might have been avoided had the appropriate action been taken earlier.

Detailed investigations into the distinguishing characteristics of failing companies were first carried out in the United States in the 1930s and 1940s, probably instigated by the New York Stock

Exchange crash of October 1929. Research concluded that the accounting ratio measurements of failing companies are significantly different from those of continuing ones. Using this basic premise, researchers, including Edward Altman, have developed failure prediction models based on accounting ratios calculated from companies' financial statements.

Three types of analysis which can be applied to a company and its financial statements are examined in this chapter. First, *traditional ratio analysis*, which is then taken a stage further to look at *multivariate ratio analysis* in the form of Z-score models as predictors of company failure. *A-score analysis* is also included as a non-financial company assessment technique.

Traditional ratio analysis is fairly commonly used by analysts and businesses alike to interpret financial statements. Failure prediction models are not widely used by businesses, accountants or analysts, although it has been demonstrated that certain models have a high success rate in identifying companies which are likely to fail. Used on a regular basis, a model can also be used as an indicator of financial trends within a business.

Whilst the statistical derivation of failure prediction models is complex, they are simple to use if the appropriate accounting data is available and can become valuable management tools, as can traditional ratio analysis, if used intelligently. As with any form of statistical analysis, the results will only be of practical use to a business or analyst if:

- the underlying data, i.e. the accounts on which the ratios are based, are reliable;
- they are analysed in conjunction with past results and future plans for the business;
- they are communicated in an intelligible fashion to those who have control over day-to-day and longer-term decision-making.

In contrast to statistical analysis, potential business problems can be identified by a technique developed by John Argenti, the 'A-score', in which scores are allocated for management, financial management and operating issues. Argenti devised a list of the factors which commonly feature in a declining business, and allocated a score to each factor according to its significance. The more factors which are observable in the business, the higher the score achieved. Scores are then assessed in conjunction with guidelines provided by Argenti. This form of analysis is necessarily subjective, given that it requires judgements on the quality of a company's management team, as well as a fairly detailed knowledge of that company. For the former reason in particular, A-score analysis tends to yield most valuable results when applied by external analysts.

## Univariate ratio analysis

A basic statistical technique for the analysis of financial statements and management accounts is univariate ratio analysis. The term 'univariate' simply refers to the fact that the accounting ratios are considered in isolation, and not combined with other ratios as is the case with failure prediction models. Ratio analysis is probably the most common technique for analysing and comparing companies' financial statements, and for making predictions of future performance based on past results.

Assuming that reliable accounts are available, a business owner or manager can conduct ratio analysis with reasonable ease. What is important is to understand what the ratios mean and assistance from the business's accountant might be initially useful to determine which ratios are appropriate and how to interpret them.

Any number of ratios can be calculated from a company's accounts, and care should always be taken to ensure that analysis is not carried out for its own sake: a page of figures means nothing without some form of commentary, conclusions and recommendations for action. Ideally, ratios should be compared with prior years' results so that declines or improvements can be identified and, if necessary, acted upon. Where there is no dedicated finance team with the time and resources available to carry out the analysis, this may seem an unnecessarily time-consuming exercise for the business owner or manager. However, once appropriate ratios have been identified, ratio analysis can be performed quickly and with no more sophisticated equipment than a basic calculator.

Accounting ratios are usually divided into three broad categories, analysing

- short-term solvency
- long-term solvency or 'financing'
- financial performance.

Summary accounts for two companies are presented below, to illustrate the accounting ratios discussed.

Initially, the profit and loss account for both companies gives an impression of a successful trading period, with earnings before interest and tax representing 8.6 per cent and 6 per cent of turnover for Companies 1 and 2 respectively. Whilst the

|  | Company 1 £'000 | Company 2 £'000 |
|---|---|---|
| *Profit and loss account* | | |
| Sales | 3,269 | 2,819 |
| Cost of goods sold | 2,440 | 144 |
| Earnings before interest and tax | 280 | 170 |
| Interest | 22 | 48 |
| *Balance sheet* | | |
| Tangible fixed assets | **73** | **784** |
| Current assets | | |
| Stock | 206 | 20 |
| Debtors | 729 | 789 |
| Cash | | 63 |
|  | 935 | 872 |
| Current liabilities | 701 | 1,250 |
| Net Current assets / (liabilities) | **234** | **(378)** |
| Creditors due after more than one year | 16 | 198 |
| Provisions | 4 | 11 |
|  | 20 | 209 |
| Net Assets | **287** | **197** |
| Capital and Reserves | | |
| Share capital | 75 | 15 |
| Profit and loss account | 212 | 182 |
|  | **287** | **197** |

companies are operating in different markets with varying industry 'norms', these results appear reasonable. A look at the balance sheet presents a different picture: Company 2 has net current liabilities of £378,000 and is technically insolvent. Although it has fixed assets of £784,000 compared with only £73,000 in Company 1, the latter company still demonstrates a stronger long-term financial position with a balance sheet total of £287,000 compared with Company 2's total of £197,000.

When looking at a set of accounts, a certain amount of information can be derived from the figures alone – whether the business is profitable, whether it is solvent and so on. However, ratio analysis can add a further dimension to the figures by providing information such as how quickly stocks are sold, how soon customers pay, how soon the business pays its suppliers and so on. Ratio analysis is therefore discussed at some length, since it can provide the business owner or manager with a considerably more detailed picture of business performance than a set of accounts alone can offer.

## Short-term solvency

Short-term solvency is critical for smaller companies, and is often a significant factor in company failure, where a sudden shortage of cash can result in disaster very quickly. Measures of short-term solvency indicate both the ability of a company to meet its immediate debts to short-term creditors and the rate at which short-term assets such as stocks and work-in-progress are converted into cash.

There are a number of ratios popularly used for measuring short-term solvency, and perhaps the most common and simple measure is the current ratio. The current ratio is calculated as

$$\frac{\text{Current assets}}{\text{Current liabilities}}$$

and is used as a measurement of working capital, or the funds available to support day-to-day trading activities, such as payments to creditors for goods purchased for resale.

For Companies 1 and 2, the result of the calculation is:

Company 1 $\dfrac{935}{701}$ = 1.33    Company 2 $\dfrac{872}{1,250}$ = 0.70

Technically, Company 2 is insolvent, that is, the current ratio is less than 1.0, and indicates that it has sufficient liquid funds available to meet only 70 per cent of its immediate debts. This technical insolvency may be a temporary condition, but should be regarded as a warning sign of potential future financial difficulties.

To be technically solvent, a business should have a current ratio in excess of 1.0. If the ratio is less than 1.0, the implication is that the business is unable to satisfy its immediate debts. A very high current ratio may not be a good one, however. A high level of cash in a manufacturing company, for example, may indicate that resources are not being used as efficiently as they could be. Perhaps the cash would be better used if invested in new machinery which could help to generate additional turnover for the company.

An alternative to the current ratio is the 'quick ratio', sometimes known as the acid test, which excludes the value of stock from the current ratio calculation.

Company 1 $\dfrac{729}{701}$ = 1.04    Company 2 $\dfrac{852}{1,250}$ = 0.68

The exclusion of stock from the ratio has a far greater impact on Company 1 for which the sale of goods is clearly its core business, which does not appear to be the case for Company 2. The ratio is therefore of limited value for Company 2. Company 1 is still solvent, but should take care to ensure that its short-term solvency position does not decline.

Although popular, these ratios should be interpreted with care, as they can be distorted by, for example, the overvaluation of stocks which may not be readily convertible into cash, or the overstatement of debtors, some of which may prove to be 'bad'. The quick ratio goes some way to eliminating these problems, but it has still been criticized on the grounds that a high level of debtors which may contribute to a healthy ratio can conceal inefficiency in managing debt-collection, for example. This can be checked by calculating the debt-collection period, which is discussed below.

The second type of short-term solvency ratio examines the rates at which short-term assets are used to generate cash. They may also be considered as measurements of management's efficiency in running the company's day-to-day operations. The most common ratios used in this context are the stock turnover period and the debt-collection period. Stock turnover is measured as

$$\frac{\text{Cost of goods sold}}{\text{Average stock held}}$$

Assuming that the stock value shown in the balance sheet is representative of average stocks held during the period, the results for the two companies are:

Company 1   $\dfrac{2,440}{206} = 11.84$   Company 2   $\dfrac{144}{20} = 7.2$

The stock-holding period for each company can be converted into days as follows:

Company 1   365 / 11.84   = 31 days      Company 2   365 / 7.2   = 51 days

Superficially, Company 1 appears to have achieved a greater degree of efficiency in its stock cycle, with stocks being held for an average of 31 days before they are sold. However, the profit and loss account for Company 2 implies that the sale of goods represents only a small proportion of its activities, and the ratio may be of only limited value for this company.

Again, the stock turnover ratio is subject to problems. While it is obviously preferable to use an average value of stock held during the period under consideration, this data may not be readily available if regular stock counts are not carried out. The valuation of stock in itself is a difficult area, particularly if a company operates in a high technology market where its products may quickly fall prey to obsolescence as technology advances. Obsolescence can be a problem in any company, however; it is easy to include in a stock valuation product lines for which, say, demand is greatly reduced, and which may not be stocked in the future. Unless there is a reasonable prospect that these items will be sold, their valuation should be written down to the amount which they will realistically realize.

Clearly, different industries will have differing average stock turnover periods. However, a company which monitors its own stock turnover regularly may detect useful indicators of potential obsolescence, increasing competition or growing demand, for example, and be in a position to take remedial action to respond to changing market conditions. Clearly, this analysis should be undertaken in conjunction with a regular review of sales by product line, so that future purchases of stock can be assessed, and cash or credit is not tied up in purchases of stocks which are unlikely to be sold reasonably quickly.

The debt-collection period is of paramount importance to all companies, particularly in a time of difficult economic conditions, when customers are likely to stretch credit terms beyond their agreed limits. The debt-collection period is measured as:

$$\frac{\text{Trade debtors} \times 365}{\text{Credit sales}}$$

and for Companies 1 and 2 are calculated as:

Company 1 $\quad \dfrac{729 \times 365}{3,269} \quad = 81 \text{ days}$ Company 2 $\quad \dfrac{789 \times 365}{2,819} \quad = 102 \text{ days}$

In both cases, and particularly for Company 2, it would appear that debt-collection is not managed efficiently. The debt-collection period should be considered in conjunction with the company's credit policy and also with prior periods' results. A rough guide used by some credit agencies is that the average age of debts should be not more than $1\frac{1}{3}$ times the company's credit period.

In the case of Company 1, if it offers credit terms of 60 days, it should not expect its debt-collection period to exceed 80 days. In the light of this information, 81 days appears more reasonable, but the company should take care to ensure that if anything, action is taken to reduce the debt-collection period, and that it is not allowed to increase any further.

The speed with which companies are able to collect their debts will to a degree depend on its position of power relative to its customers. Some small companies suffer particularly badly because debtors know that their custom is important to that company. Conversely, larger companies are often able to dictate stringent credit terms to their customers, so that in both cases the smaller, less powerful company is left in a very weak cash position. It has to suffer breaches of credit terms by its larger customers, while having to adhere to the credit terms of its larger suppliers.

## Long-term solvency

Long-term solvency ratios measure the financial stability of a company over a longer period, and its ability to meet all debts including those which are not yet payable. These would include amounts such as long-term loans.

A useful measure of long-term solvency is the shareholders' equity ratio, which is measured as:

$$\frac{\text{Shareholders' equity} \times 100}{\text{Total assets}}$$

For Companies 1 and 2, the results of the calculation are:

Company 1 $\quad \dfrac{287}{1,008} \times 100 \quad = 28.5\%$ Company 2 $\quad \dfrac{197}{1,656} \times 100 \quad = 11.9\%$

Shareholders' equity includes ordinary share capital and the accumulated profit or loss of the company. The lower the percentage, the higher the dependence of the company on external sources of finance such as loans rather than share capital. The ratio tends to be of more relevance to publicly quoted companies, where fluctuating net profit levels can affect dividend payments to shareholders and thereby affect the quoted share price. However, it is useful as an indicator of the relative dependence on internal and external sources of long-term finance. It is usually felt that the lower the degree of dependence on external finance, the stronger the financial position of the company is likely to be in the long term.

In small and privately owned companies, it is generally the case that in the early years or during a period of expansion, there is a high degree of reliance on external sources of funds, usually bank loan facilities and credit terms granted by suppliers of goods and services. The percentage for such companies are therefore likely to be relatively low, as is the case for both companies here.

The interest coverage ratio is also of importance in assessing a company's long-term financial stability, because an inability to meet regular interest payments on short- and long-term debt can endanger a company's existence: if interest payments are not met, the loan is soon likely to be called in. The interest coverage ratio is measured by:

$$\frac{\text{Profit before interest and tax}}{\text{Interest charges for the period}}$$

Company 1 $\quad \dfrac{280}{22} \quad = 12.7$ times $\quad$ Company 2 $\quad \dfrac{170}{48} \quad = 3.5$ times

Both companies are comfortably able to meet their interest charges: broadly, if the charges can be covered three times over, analysts would regard the company as a reasonable long-term risk.

## Financial performance

Financial performance can be assessed by asset turnover ratios which measure the efficiency with which assets are used by management to generate revenue. High asset turnovers indicate that assets are being utilized efficiently. Two ratios are considered especially useful: the *total asset turnover ratio* and the *fixed asset turnover ratio*.

Total asset turnover is measured by:

$$\frac{\text{Turnover}}{\text{Total assets}}$$

Company 1 $\quad \dfrac{3,269}{1,008} \quad = 3.2$ times $\quad$ Company 2 $\quad \dfrac{2,819}{1,656} \quad = 1.7$ times

Fixed asset turnover is measured by

$$\frac{\text{Turnover}}{\text{Fixed assets}}$$

Company 1 $\quad \dfrac{3,269}{73} \quad = 44.8$ times $\quad$ Company 2 $\quad \dfrac{2,819}{784} \quad = 3.6$ times

Company 1 appears to have a remarkably high fixed asset turnover ratio, but this should be interpreted with care. It may be that the company owns no property and little plant and machinery, as might be the case with a distribution or service company, and in this context, the ratio is clearly of very limited value. The ratio is of most value to companies which own fixed assets which are directly utilized in the company's operations, the most obvious example being manufacturing plant and machinery.

The most commonly used measure of financial performance is the return on capital employed. It can be expressed in a number of ways, one of the most useful being as a return on net assets, calculated as:

$$\frac{\text{Profit before interest and tax}}{\text{Total assets less current liabilities}} \times 100$$

Company 1 $\dfrac{280 \times 100}{307} = 91.2\%$  Company 2 $\dfrac{170 \times 100}{406} = 41.8\%$

The ratio measures the degree of efficiency with which management have utilized the company's resources to generate profits, and Company 1 demonstrates an extremely high degree of efficiency. Again, the low level of fixed assets held by the company may contribute to this result.

An alternative to return on capital employed ratio is the net profit to net worth ratio, which is measured as:

$$\frac{\text{Profit before interest and tax}}{\text{Total assets less total liabilities}}$$

Company 1 $\dfrac{280}{1,008 - 721} = 0.98$  Company 2 $\dfrac{170}{1,656 - 1,459} = 0.86$

The ratio is similar to the return on capital employed calculation, but also includes long-term liabilities. The comparatively high long-term liabilities shown in the balance sheet of Company 2 lead to a significant decrease in the variation between the ratios for the two companies.

Numerous other ratios can be computed from a company's financial statements or management accounts, but care should always be exercised to ensure that they are appropriate to the company and industry under observation. As an exercise in interpreting financial and solvency trends exhibited by a company, ratio analysis can provide valuable indications of future performance.

In the prediction of company failure, univariate ratio analysis has a useful but limited role, and analysts have reached differing conclusions as to those ratios which are most valuable as predictors. John Argenti has also enumerated some of the restrictions of ratio analysis.

First, while ratio analysis over an extended period may provide indications that a company is experiencing difficulties, or is likely to in the future, it cannot provide concrete evidence of the likelihood of company failure or when it might occur.

The results of ratio analysis may be restricted by the effects of inflation. The historic cost of fixed assets, for example, may provide increasingly misleading results when applied in an asset turnover ratio. What may appear to be an improving ratio may be the opposite in real terms.

Finally, when the management of a company become aware that it is facing financial difficulties, there is a tendency for 'creative accounting' to take place to hide the true position of the company. Stocks may be overvalued, or bad debts understated, for example, to improve both the profit and loss account and balance sheet. Invoices from suppliers of goods and services may not be recorded with the intention of querying them at a later date. Such creative accounting is one of the main reasons why a failing company may appear perfectly healthy, and its difficulties may remain largely hidden until its insolvency is announced. From the viewpoint of the company itself, creative accounting brings no real benefits at all: concealing financial difficulties will not solve them, even if they remain hidden from third parties longer than they would otherwise have done.

This proved to be the case for a small family-owned limited company which manufactured transformers. Historically, the company showed excellent results, and following his retirement, the managing director planned to sell the company. While orders had tailed off somewhat, financial performance appeared to be holding up well, judging from management accounts prepared by the company's accountant.

An enthusiastic potential buyer was found, who sensibly waited until audited financial statements had been prepared before making any final decision about the purchase. In fact, the audit revealed serious problems which had previously gone undetected.

Stocks had been purchased specifically for a large order which had subsequently fallen through and could not be adapted for any other use. No provision had been made to write down the value of these stocks. In addition, it emerged that this same customer was suffering financial difficulties, and that invoices dating back to some six months earlier remained unpaid – and with little prospect of receiving full payment in the foreseeable future. No provision had been made against these potentially bad debts. The audited accounts ultimately presented a picture of a company whose performance and stability had deteriorated considerably compared with previous years, and with a managing director who appeared unable to acknowledge its problems even to himself.

Discussions with the buyer came to an abrupt end at this stage: perhaps not surprisingly, he had received no prior warning of these problems and now could not be confident that others would not emerge later. The basis of trust on which the negotiations had previously been conducted was destroyed, and he had no further contact with the company.

## Multivariate ratio analysis

The difference between univariate and multivariate ratio analysis is that the latter combines a series of weighted accounting ratios to give an aggregate 'score' for a company. The score is interpreted in conjunction with pre-set limits which define whether the company is likely to continue trading or fail. In this respect, the analysis is also known as *discriminant analysis*, whereby the goal is to identify the distinguishing characteristics of two or more distinct populations, in this case failing and continuing companies.

Edward Altman is one of the leading authorities in the field, and has formulated a 'Z-score' model for publicly quoted companies which claims a predictive success rate of 95 per cent and 72 per cent, one and two financial statements prior to failure respectively, although this falls to 48 per cent three financial statements prior to failure. This is hardly surprising, given that the signs of failure will become more evident in a company's financial statements as failure approaches. Obviously, the sooner potential failure can be highlighted, the more likely it is that managers are able to take action to attempt to reverse the declining trend.

Less research has been devoted to formulating an equivalent model for privately owned companies, but Edward Altman is again amongst those to have done so. His model achieved a predictive success rate of 94 per cent one financial statement prior to failure.

Obviously, Z-score analysis is subject to the same problems as traditional ratio analysis. Additionally, most of the research carried out to test the success rate of the model has used ex-post data, that is, has analysed failures after the event.

The use of the model as a management tool to aid decision-making or to predict events is still uncommon. A further problem is that although the model may predict failure, it cannot predict when failure will occur. However, if it draws attention sufficiently early to the fact that a potential problem exists, companies can attempt to take remedial action to avoid failure. Of course, such action will not be effective in all cases, but if the warning signs are heeded, there may be some companies for which predicted failure need not become a reality.

As with traditional ratio analysis, the business owner or manager should be able to calculate a Z-score based on the business's accounts. While the formula may look daunting, it is mainly a question of extracting figures from a set of accounts and slotting them into the equation.

The model as formulated by Edward Altman for private companies contains the following data:

| Variable | Ratio | Weight |
|---|---|---|
| $X_1$ | $\dfrac{\text{Working capital}}{\text{Total assets}}$ | 0.717 |
| $X_2$ | $\dfrac{\text{Retained earnings}}{\text{Total assets}}$ | 0.847 |

$X_3$    $\dfrac{\text{Earnings before interest and taxation}}{\text{Total assets}}$    3.107

$X_4$    $\dfrac{\text{Book value of net worth}}{\text{Total liabilities}}$    0.420

$X_5$    $\dfrac{\text{Sales}}{\text{Total assets}}$    0.998

$X_1$   Working capital is the difference between current assets and current liabilities. Total assets is the sum of fixed assets and current assets.

$X_2$   Retained earnings is the total of profits and losses over the whole life of the company, as shown by the balance sheet.

$X_3$   Earnings before interest and taxation is the figure for net profit in the profit and loss account, excluding interest and taxation.

$X_4$   Book value of net worth is the combined book value of all classes of share. Total liabilities is the sum of current liabilities and long-term liabilities.

The cut-off points for non-failing and failing companies are as follows. A score of 2.9 or more classifies a company as non-failing. A score of 1.23 or less classifies a company as failing. A score falling between 1.23 and 2.9 puts a company in the grey area or zone of ignorance, because of the level of classification errors which occur in this range.

The equation for calculating the Z-score is expressed as:

$$Z = (X_1 \times 0.717) + (X_2 \times 0.847) + (X_3 \times 3.107) + (X_4 \times 0.420) + (X_5 \times 0.998)$$

The Z-scores for Companies 1 and 2 are calculated as follows:

| | Company 1 | | | Company 2 | | |
|---|---|---|---|---|---|---|
| $X_1$ | $\dfrac{(935 - 701)}{(73 + 935)}$ | $\times\ 0.717$ | $= 0.166$ | $\dfrac{(872 - 1{,}250)}{(784 + 872)}$ | $\times\ 0.717$ | $= -0.164$ |
| $X_2$ | $\dfrac{212}{(73 + 935)}$ | $\times\ 0.847$ | $= 0.178$ | $\dfrac{182}{(784 + 872)}$ | $\times\ 0.847$ | $= 0.093$ |
| $X_3$ | $\dfrac{280}{(73 + 935)}$ | $\times\ 3.107$ | $= 0.863$ | $\dfrac{170}{(784 + 872)}$ | $\times\ 3.107$ | $= 0.319$ |
| $X_4$ | $\dfrac{75}{(701 + 20)}$ | $\times\ 0.420$ | $= 0.044$ | $\dfrac{15}{(1{,}250 + 209)}$ | $\times\ 0.420$ | $= 0.004$ |
| $X_5$ | $\dfrac{3{,}269}{(73 + 935)}$ | $\times\ 0.998$ | $= 3.237$ | $\dfrac{2{,}819}{(784 + 872)}$ | $\times\ 0.998$ | $= 1.700$ |
| Z-score | | **4.488** | | | **1.952** | |

The Z-score for Company 1 falls safely above the cut-off point of 2.9 for non-failing companies and would be considered to be not at risk. Company 2, on the other hand, falls within the grey area which covers the range 1.23 to 2.9. It could not be classified conclusively as at risk, but it is likely that there is cause for concern. If the Z-score were to decline in later periods, it should be regarded as a warning sign that positive action is required if failure is to be avoided.

There are problems associated with the classification of companies on the basis of their Z-score, particularly in the case of private companies where significantly less research has been carried out to validate the test results obtained by Altman.

Furthermore, if a company is relatively young, its Z-score can show worse prospects for the future than may actually be the case. For example, variable $X_2$ implicitly considers the age of the company, in that retained earnings are included in the equation. If a company is young and has not yet built up its cumulative profits, it will probably achieve a poor result for variable $X_2$. It could be argued that young companies become subject to unfair discrimination, but this does reflect reality: a company is much more likely to fail in the early years of its existence. This does not mean that a poor Z-score for a company which has been trading for less than, say, five years should be dismissed automatically as a rogue result.

The context in which Z-score results are interpreted is extremely important. The test should be applied to financial statements covering a number of financial periods in order to establish a trend in the company's solvency pattern. The value of the interpretation will be further enhanced if scores are compared with those of other companies in the same market sector, and ideally with an industry 'norm'. Clearly, such information will not always be easily obtainable, particularly for private companies.

It should also be remembered that comparison of Z-scores for companies within different market sectors may yield misleading results. This also raises the question of the applicability of a single model to companies operating in manufacturing, wholesaling, retailing and service sectors and to companies of varying sizes.

The development of separate models to take account of these factors would undoubtedly improve the validity of the Z-score results.

In spite of these potential drawbacks, the Z-score model is a management tool which has a useful role alongside traditional ratio analysis in the interpretation of a company's financial results – if used intelligently.

A problem of a different nature which exists in any form of business analysis is the reaction to the results of the analysis by the directors, shareholders or owners of the business, particularly in the case of small, privately owned companies.

The human factor frequently dictates that predictions of poor results for the future are greeted with disbelief, largely through a lack of detailed understanding of their implications. One common misconception is that if current and anticipated future sales are at a satisfactory level, then the business will somehow automatically continue to trade successfully and generate sufficient cash inflows to meet all liabilities as they fall due. In practice, this is not necessarily the case and if, say, gross profit margins have been cut to stimulate sales and / or debtors are slow in paying, serious cashflow problems can quickly result.

This might be the case for Company 2 above. Although the company is generating profits, it is technically insolvent. If the debt-collection period could be reduced to, say, 60 days, additional cash of some £326,000 could have been generated with which to meet the company's current liabilities. The company would still be technically insolvent, but the amount by which current liabilities exceed current assets would be reduced to £52,000 from £378,000. While still not an entirely satisfactory state of affairs, this would represent a significant improvement in the company's short-term financial stability.

An additional associated problem is the highly sensitive nature of Z-score analysis: business owners or managers may well prefer poor results to remain confidential in order not to undermine confidence in the business, both internally and externally. This might apply in particular to employees who may become concerned for the security of their jobs if aware that a business may fail. Policy for this type of issue will obviously vary from business to business – some choose to communicate details of financial performance to employees, others do not.

An issue which is rarely covered in discussions of Z-score analysis is how to improve the Z-score and reduce the chances of failure. The main reason for this is the impossibility of setting down hard and fast rules for the improvement of business performance. This is true particularly when broader economic factors are unfavourable and businesses are struggling against the problems caused by a downturn in demand and severe price competition.

Depending on the level of financial expertise available within the business, the most constructive course of action is to analyse why performance has declined, either in-house or with the assistance of an external adviser.

Assuming that management accounts are available, this is a good starting point. If not, accounting books and records – cash book, sales and purchase day books, stock listings and so on – can be analysed to determine the areas of the business which have contributed to the decline. These may include decreasing sales, lower sales prices, higher suppliers' prices, slower debt-collection or an increase in bad debts – to name some of the more common factors.

How the business attempts to remedy its problems in any given area will vary between businesses, and, for some, winding up may be the conclusion. However, strategies for improving control over financial and accounting issues are discussed in chapter 5.

## A-score

The A-score technique for predicting company failure was developed by John Argenti. In 1983 he cited a survey conducted by Dun and Bradstreet in 1973, concluding that 93 per cent of company failures result from managerial incompetence: the remaining 7 per cent are accounted for by neglect, fraud and disaster. The survey results may hold no surprises for some analysts, but business owners and managers often underestimate the importance of the effects of their actions and decisions on the future existence of their company, compared with the importance of external factors.

The two most significant aspects of managerial incompetence identified by Dun and Bradstreet are the failure to secure adequate sales and competitive weakness. Argenti goes on to examine the management characteristics and resulting company defects which are likely to lead to company failure. Scores are allocated to a number of Defects, Mistakes and Symptoms, which are weighted in accordance with the importance of their contribution to the failure process.

## DEFECTS, MISTAKES, SYMPTOMS AND THEIR SCORES

| *Defects* | *Score* |
|---|---|
| Autocrat | 8 |
| Chairman and Chief Executive | 4 |
| Passive Board | 2 |
| Unbalanced skills | 2 |
| Weak Finance Director | 2 |
| Poor management depth | 1 |
| No budgetary control | 3 |
| No cashflow plans | 3 |
| No costing system | 3 |
| Poor response to change | 15 |
| **Maximum total for Defects** | **43** |
| Pass mark for Defects | 10 |

| *Mistakes* | |
|---|---|
| High gearing | 15 |
| Overtrading | 15 |
| Big project | 15 |
| **Maximum total for Mistakes** | **45** |
| Pass mark for Mistakes | 15 |

*Symptoms*

| | |
|---|---|
| Financial signs | 4 |
| Creative accounting | 4 |
| Non-financial signs | 3 |
| Terminal signs | 1 |
| Maximum total for Symptoms | 12 |
| Maximum total overall | 100 |
| Pass mark overall | 25 |

Source: J. Argenti, 'Predicting Corporate Failure', *Accountants'*
*Digest*, No. 138 (ICAEW, 1983).

## Defects

The first group of Defects is concerned with problems in management structure. The 'autocrat' refers to a dominating personality, an individual who may take decisions without heeding the advice or wishes of colleagues or advisers. Although it may be difficult to draw a distinction between an autocrat and a strong leader, the former is likely to feature in a business which has reached the size where it would be more effectively run by a team than by an individual. A distinction also needs to be drawn between autocracy and a one-man band. A small business run by, say, a husband and wife team or by a single individual should not be confused with an autocratic leader. However, the same symptoms may still be visible in smaller businesses.

'Chairman and Chief Executive' describes a similar situation, and again is less likely to occur in a smaller business. Where one individual fulfils the roles of both Chairman and Chief Executive, there is once more a danger that the decision-making process will be dominated by the views of only that individual.

A 'Passive Board' is a situation which can easily arise where an autocrat is present in the business at a senior level. It may be that other members of the board have a particular interest in specific areas of the business only, or that they are representatives of lending institutions who take little active role in the management of the business.

Similarly, unbalanced skills are most likely to be visible in a business where an autocrat wishes to retain maximum control. The skills refer not only to those of the directors, but also to those of senior management who could play a significant role in formulating business decisions. Argenti quotes as a common scenario the engineering company where most of the board, including the autocratic Chief Executive, are engineers. The chances of decisions initiated by the Chief Executive being challenged are thus reduced dramatically. The most significant danger is that a board which does not contain a balanced range of skills will be less able to respond effectively to problems or opportunities which arise.

A weak Finance Director, or a finance function which is not represented at board level presents a similar problem. Whether accountancy information and business performance are good or bad, these matters do require informed discussion by the board.

While Argenti is less than convinced of the importance of a lack of management depth as a factor in business failure, it can undoubtedly affect the operation of a business. A highly effective board of directors cannot necessarily run a successful business without support from managers, team leaders, supervisors and so on.

The second group of Defects is concerned with accounting information. Budgetary control, cashflow forecasts and costing systems all provide the information required to monitor business performance effectively. While it may be clear without this type of information that problems exist within the business, it will be far more difficult to determine where the problem originated and therefore what action should be taken. A lack of accounting information is also likely to be a result of poor management.

Finally in the group of Defects is 'Poor response to change'. This might refer to changes in market requirements, in the economy, in technology or in other factors which adversely affect the business. For example, a business which expends considerable resources developing a high-tech product but which does not monitor the products developed by its competitors can find itself overtaken and lose its niche in the market. A well-managed business will not only be aware of the dangers of change, but will also be able to respond positively and quickly.

Although many of the Defects listed above may seem to be applicable only to larger companies, the same principles apply to all businesses. For example, the sole trader who takes no notice of valuable guidance offered by external advisers because it is not 'convenient' is falling into the same trap as the autocratic Chief Executive.

## Mistakes

High gearing, overtrading and the big project are all discussed in chapter 2, and all three can be significant factors in business decline. Again, it can be argued that in a well-managed business, the resulting problems should be recognized at a sufficiently early stage for some remedial action – or at least damage limitation – to be undertaken.

## Symptoms

'Financial signs' are among the more obvious indicators of decline in a business. Accounts, assuming they present a fair picture, and ratio analysis should reveal the problem areas if these have not already become evident.

However, if creative accounting has taken place, these signs will be less obvious. There are many techniques for distorting a business's trading results or balance sheet position, but the most significant point here is that trouble has been taken to present a misleading set of accounts. The motivation behind creative accounting may not be overtly fraudulent in the mind of the preparer of the accounts or the business owner, but may be felt to be justified in order to keep the business afloat – to persuade a bank manager to renew overdraft facilities, for example. It is also a sure sign that the business owner has recognized that the future of the business is in jeopardy.

'Non-financial signs' of decline may become obvious only on a piecemeal basis and can cover a whole variety of factors. These may range from a deliberate reduction in stock levels or unexpected redundancies to the increasingly shabby appearance of offices. Few parties are likely to be aware of all of these factors in a larger company, although in smaller businesses the signs will be more clear.

'Terminal signs' of failure tend to occur very shortly before the collapse of a business. Increasing numbers of creditors are threatening legal action, the bank manager is constantly seeking assurances that the overdraft limit will not be breached again, bailiffs are at the door to collect arrears of VAT, creditors refuse to supply any further goods – the list goes on. When these events are occurring with increasing frequency and in increasing number, collapse may be inevitable.

The allocation and interpretation of scores is a straightforward exercise. Either the full score or nil should be allocated for each category; no intermediate scores are permitted. Scores should be allocated only if there is confidence that items are 'clearly visible in the suspect company'. The overall pass mark is 25, and any company achieving a greater score is considered to exhibit so many of the signs which frequently precede failure that serious concern is advised.

A company which scores above the pass mark in any individual category should also be regarded with circumspection. If, for example, it scores less than 10 for Defects but more than 15 for Mistakes, this might indicate that while the management team is fundamentally competent, it is taking risks with the future of the company, either knowingly or otherwise.

To demonstrate how A-score analysis is applied, the failed companies described in chapter 2 – Data Magnetics, Sinclair Research and Rolls-Royce – are analysed below. It should be stressed that the scores are subject to the benefits of hindsight, but also subject to an inability to observe first-hand the companies as they were and for this reason they should be regarded largely as illustrative. However, they do provide an insight into how scores might be allocated.

In each case, scores have been allocated only where the factor is very obviously present, and the scores indicate how easily a company can exceed the pass mark of 25.

All three companies have been allocated scores for both

| | Data Magnetics | Sinclair Research | Rolls-Royce |
|---|---|---|---|
| *Defects* | | | |
| Autocrat | – | 8 | – |
| Chairman & Chief Executive | – | – | – |
| Passive Board | – | – | – |
| Unbalanced skills | – | – | – |
| Weak Finance Director | – | – | – |
| Poor management depth | – | – | – |
| No budgetary control | 3 | – | 3 |
| No cashflow plans | – | – | 3 |
| No costing system | – | – | 3 |
| Poor response to change | 15 | 15 | 15 |
| Sub-total | **18** | **23** | **24** |
| *Mistakes* | | | |
| High leverage | – | – | – |
| Overtrading | – | – | – |
| Big project | 15 | 15 | 15 |
| Sub-total | **15** | **15** | **15** |
| *Symptoms* | | | |
| Financial signs | 4 | 4 | 4 |
| Creative accounting | – | – | – |
| Non-financial signs | 3 | 3 | 3 |
| Terminal signs | – | 1 | – |
| Sub-total | **7** | **8** | **7** |
| **Grand total** | **40** | **46** | **46** |

'Poor response to change' and 'Big project'. This is justified on the following grounds.

Data Magnetics entered into a project which required vast injections of capital and technical resources in a high-risk market at a time of constant change. The company was based solely around this project, which was attempting to break new ground. It is interesting to note that had the time scale for the development of the product been shorter, the company may well have become highly profitable very quickly.

Sinclair Research – or rather Clive Sinclair – falls into these categories because he was not prepared to sacrifice any element of his role as an innovator to the financial well-being of his company. This was particularly dangerous since it was a time in the mid-1980s when competitors' products were beginning to overtake Sinclair's in terms of quality and price. His 'Big project' was his propensity to invest resources – both his own and the company's – in continuing programmes of research into new products and markets, to the detriment of the development of existing ones, which led to a fatal imbalance in the company.

In Rolls-Royce's case, the management of the RB211 contract displayed evidence of a lack of response to the ever more competitive conditions within this market. The lack of financial control over the 'Big project' which was to cause the downfall of the company stemmed from outmoded organizational and financial systems, which might have been adequate decades earlier, but were so no longer. An interesting point in the subsequent operations of the company is that during the early 1980s the company made substantial investment in new plant and machinery in an attempt to reduce production costs. This was a further 'Big project' which could have backfired – but this time the gamble paid off.

Again, small, young companies which are both owned and managed by one or two individuals may appear to be discriminated against. They may well achieve high scores in both the Defects and Mistakes sections, especially in the early years of their existence. Although this may seem unfair, these companies are generally at greater risk than older, more established ones, particularly in periods of poor economic conditions.

Identifying practical solutions to remedy the areas of management weakness highlighted by A-score analysis poses a further problem. In a larger company, it might be feasible to replace or add to the management team to provide new expertise. In a smaller company, this is unlikely to be a workable option for several reasons. First, where the management of the company is largely undertaken by one individual, he or she may be unwilling to relinquish the day-to-day control they have become accustomed to. Next, the cost of employing an experienced manager may be too great for the company reasonably to contemplate in a period of difficult trading conditions. Finally, and perhaps most commonly, there is the case where a company is both owned and managed by the same individual who relies on external specialists for professional support. It may well be perceived that to take on an employee to manage these activities presents the owner-manager with more problems than it solves in terms of identifying a suitable candidate, allocating and supervising work and maintaining consistency of business practice.

The highly subjective nature of this form of analysis makes it difficult for business owners or managers to apply it to their own company. It will be of more value if scores are allocated by an external observer who can view the company impartially and make reasonably scientific judgements as to its weaknesses. It also relies on a fairly detailed knowledge of the company and those who manage it; allocating scores on the basis of second-hand information rather than on first-hand experience will probably yield misleading scores.

However, the business owner or manager is the individual who can derive greatest benefit from the analysis, and with the possible exception of the Symptoms sections, should be able to make a reasonable analysis of the business.

This type of information is also likely to be taken into account by banks and other lenders, overtly or not, in assessing the overall health of a business. While they may not conduct such a structured analysis, they will look at the quality of management, the availability of financial information and the overall conduct of the business's operations.

Similarly, employees – current or potential – might implicitly use these factors in weighing up the future prospects of a business. When competition for jobs is fierce, it may be that individuals are simply relieved to be in employment, and do not look too carefully at the quality of the business. However, in the event that alternative job opportunities are on offer, A-score analysis can offer potential employees a framework for assessing aspects of a potential employer beyond those relating specifically to the job in question.

Clearly, on the basis of one or two meetings, it will not always be easy to judge accurately whether the Defects, Mistakes and Symptoms enumerated by Argenti are present in the business. Tactful questions will yield a certain amount of information, but an interviewer is unlikely to want to give away too many personal details about the business. In spite of this, questions might be asked about:

- the management structure of the business;
- the monitoring of financial performance and recent actual results;
- plans for the future of the business, including specific opportunities and threats;
- the business's strengths;
- how the business has developed in recent years.

While the prospective employee may not be able to undertake the thorough examination of the business required to allocate scores with a high degree of accuracy, A-score analysis can nevertheless be used as a framework for assessment.

In spite of its drawbacks, the A-score method does enjoy the advantage over purely statistical analysis that it is not entirely reliant on accounting data. This reflects the feeling of many financial analysts that whilst reliable accounting data can provide useful information about a company it can never present the full picture. Unreliable accounting data can, of course, present a worse than useless picture of a company, in that misleading conclusions can be drawn.

As with the results of Z-score analysis, the most sensitive problem for an analyst is to communicate the results to the business owner or manager, and to ensure they are understood and acted upon in the most beneficial way for the company. To ignore warnings of potential problems is a common reaction, either in the hope of concealing them from third parties or through sheer fear of the consequences. The 'head in the sand' approach to business problems may not be a constructive one, but it is often the preferred one.

## Usefulness of statistical analysis

While statistical techniques are frequently used by external analysts of a company, including accountants and bank managers, are they of practical use to the company owner or manager?

Small companies which do not have the resources to employ a full-time dedicated finance team but rely on, say, a book-keeper and external accountant to manage their financial affairs may doubt the relevance of what appears to be statistical analysis for its own sake. Analysis should be tailored to suit the needs of the company, and be conducted on a regular basis.

It is easy to fall into the trap of producing lists of ratios based on a company's financial statements without also looking at the reasons for the results obtained. For example, a gross profit margin of 25 per cent or a debt-collection period of 75 days mean nothing if they are not considered in the context of the company's projections for the current period and results for prior periods.

However, it is equally easy to fall into the trap of believing that management of the operational side of the business takes precedence over all else, and that if operations appear to be running smoothly, they will continue to do so in the future. Business owners and managers who take this passive approach to the financial management of their company are likely to be those who are unable to adapt and take remedial action when problems start to occur.

If financial problems can be anticipated by the analysis of prior periods' results so that plans for the future can be revised accordingly, techniques such as ratio analysis and Z-score analysis begin to take on a more practical and positive role. Action might take a very simple form, such as more rigorous chasing of debtors if debt-collection periods have increased unduly. It might be more far-reaching, such as a review of the company's product range to weed out those lines on which gross profit margins have decreased. Alternatively, if the company's liquidity position is declining, capital expenditure such as the replacement of company cars might be delayed to ease the drain on the company's cash and credit facilities.

It is worth stating again that the practical value to the management of a company of any form of predictive analysis depends entirely on the business owner or manager's attitude towards it. A sceptical or head in the sand approach will dictate that it is of extremely limited value.

Predictive analysis techniques can also be of help to investors and lenders in determining whether a company is a safe risk. Statistical analysis which points either to a decline in a company's financial position or to poor financial management will obviously deter a potential investor. This can be compared with a potential investor in the stock market, who is unlikely to invest in a company whose results and activities have received adverse comment from analysts in the media.

Many small companies in particular are not skilled at planning ahead and can tend to allow minor financial problems to grow out of control. What may appear a short-term cash deficit caused by delayed payment from a small number of customers can quickly become a major problem, such that liabilities for VAT and other taxes suddenly cannot be met. Except in unusual circumstances, these problems can be pre-empted, if not avoided, by keeping a watchful eye on the company's short-term liquidity position. A bank manager will generally take a far more positive attitude towards a company which maintains regular contact with the bank and gives warning of potential problems.

Making predictions about a company's future financial position in this way does not necessarily mean that failure can be avoided, and in some cases it might even hasten a decision to put the company into liquidation. The purpose of predictive analysis is to aid decision-making and to highlight areas of weakness, not to provide cures for financial or operational problems.

# 7. **Economic issues**

Throughout the late 1980s and the early 1990s, the decline of the UK domestic economy into recession became an increasingly emotive issue for businesses and individuals alike. Both consumer and business confidence were badly hit, and many small businesses in particular felt powerless to respond positively to the challenge of survival in worsening economic conditions. The point has already been made that, to a degree, these businesses were at the mercy of economic factors beyond their control, and the youngest ones which had not yet had the opportunity to build up a reasonable level of financial stability probably suffered most. The level of business failures in the early 1990s, as set out in chapter 1, is the most forceful indicator of the depth of the difficulties which faced some of these businesses.

There is little that some businesses could do to improve their chances of survival under these conditions, but many business owners and managers feel with the benefit of hindsight that they could have responded differently to broader economic considerations. They now realize to what degree the economy in the broadest sense can represent a source of external instability for any business, however well controlled that business might be.

There are many far-reaching issues which have a direct or knock-on effect on business, and especially small businesses, when economic conditions become unfavourable. It is worthwhile looking at some of the most significant ones to determine whether smaller businesses can take any positive action to mitigate any adverse effects. These include:

- interest rates
- tax policies
- inflation
- the effects of recession on expectations.

It is also worth remembering that these are matters which the business owner or manager would be wise to bear in mind regardless of economic conditions. For example, the purchase of new premises when the bank base rate has fallen considerably and the property market has been relatively stagnant may be tempting, and indeed it may be a sensible option. However, the business owner or manager should not fall into the trap of assuming that the base rate will remain low. It is one of the many factors over which the business has no control, and should always be regarded as potentially volatile.

## Interest rates

Interest rates represent the cost of credit to a borrower, and in simple terms, are often used as a tool by governments to influence the demand for credit. The table below sets out the movements in the bank base rate in recent years.

**Bank Base Rates 1988–1993**

| 1988 | 29 Jun | 9.5 | 1991 | 22 Mar | 12.5 |
|------|--------|-----|------|--------|------|
| | 5 Jul | 10.0 | | 13 Apr | 12.0 |
| | 19 Jul | 10.5 | | 25 May | 11.5 |
| | 8 Aug | 10.5–11.0 | | 13 Jul | 11.0 |
| | 9 Aug | 11.0 | | 4 Sep | 10.5 |
| | 25 Aug | 11.0–12.0 | 1992 | 5 May | 10.0 |
| | 25 Nov | 13.0 | | 17 Sep | 12.0 |
| 1989 | 24 May | 14.0 | | 18 Sep | 10.0 |
| | 5 Oct | 15.0 | | 23 Sep | 9.0 |
| 1990 | 8 Oct | 14.0 | | 15 Oct | 8.0 |
| 1991 | 14 Feb | 13.5 | | 13 Nov | 7.0 |
| | 27 Feb | 13.0 | 1993 | 26 Jan | 6.0 |

The period of over two years from November 1988 when interest rates were at 13 per cent or above coincides, not surprisingly, with the point at which both company and individual insolvencies started to increase sharply, although there was a time-lag before the worst effects began to be felt. Many businesses became more vulnerable during 1991–92, than in the period immediately after the interest rate rise. However, the effect of interest rate cuts throughout 1992 was not reflected in a corresponding decrease in the number of business failures, which continued to rise. This emphasizes the fact that although lower interest rates may be beneficial to businesses in general terms, it may be some time before these benefits are felt.

As well as this, there are businesses whose borrowings are subject to a fixed minimum lending rate, such as 3 per cent over base rate subject to a minimum of 11 per cent. A business in these circumstances would benefit from reductions in bank base rates down to 8 per cent. Below this level (i.e. 11 per cent less 3 per cent), the business will not be in a position to enjoy the benefits of further reductions, since the lending rate will remain at 11 per cent. It is probably worthwhile attempting to renegotiate the terms of the loan or overdraft, although it is likely that banks will only be prepared to carry out such a review on a fixed and pre-determined basis, often annually.

The problem of high interest rates is more complex than a simple case of additional pressures on profitability due to increased levels of interest on borrowings, in that a vicious circle is also created. For example, a retailer suffering from depressed levels of sales comes to the conclusion that, by reducing levels of stocks, borrowings and therefore interest costs can be reduced. However, the next business in the supply chain, the wholesaler, is now left with higher stock-holdings, and needs more finance to support the increased costs to the business. The wholesaler in turn cuts stock levels by reducing orders from manufacturers – who now have a need for a greater level of borrowing. To adapt to the new lower order levels, manufacturers reduce production, which may involve cutting the workforce by means of redundancies. Individuals in turn cut their spending and the whole process begins again.

This is one of the types of pressures which small businesses have had to face, in that for many, demand has fallen to the point where the business is no longer viable. Costs have been cut as far as possible, and yet the need for borrowings has not fallen sufficiently. At the same time, if expectations for the short- and medium-term future look gloomy, banks become increasingly aware of their exposure and concerned for the security of their lendings. Again, it is often the smaller business which suffers first. Although the amounts borrowed by small businesses are generally tiny compared with those of major PLCs, they are often the most risky so far as the bank is concerned.

Banks – and other institutions – have maintained throughout recessions that actions to wind up a company or bankrupt an individual in order to recover their loans have been taken only as a last resort. Both banks and other creditors often feel they have a greater chance of recovering the amounts owed to them if the business continues to trade, except in circumstances where the business has clearly failed. It can be the case that if, for example, a bank were to foreclose on borrowings, it would recover less of its money than if it allowed the business to continue to trade – at least in the short term. However, as an economy emerges from recession and businesses begin to recover, there may be an increase in the number of businesses forced into liquidation by banks, as borrowings are finally called in.

A lesson learnt by many business owners and managers – not to mention personal borrowers – from the credit boom of the mid1980s has been the danger of borrowing to excess, even when there is considerable encouragement to do so. This has been illustrated by the simple but traumatic cases of many house buyers, who took on apparently affordable mortgages when the property market was rising, but who quickly found themselves in deep financial trouble when the market slowed and interest rates began to rise.

It is easy to see these dangers in retrospect: no market will continue to rise indefinitely. In spite of this, a booming economy coupled with enormous government incentive for the setting up of small businesses and entrepreneurial spirit could not help but persuade many to take this step. Logically, businesses should have been able to foresee the dangers. However, many factors in the economy and therefore for business depend on expectations and confidence, and these are human issues which cannot be controlled scientifically, and are not always based on logical analysis.

On a more positive note, small businesses continue to be established even in poor economic circumstances. However, many of the individuals who do take this step are adamant that bank borrowings will be kept to an absolute minimum (if they manage to secure borrowings at all). There is also likely to emerge an increasing preference to provide the working capital for their enterprises from personal savings or investment by individuals, in order to avoid the risks of borrowing altogether, at least in the initial set-up and trading period when the dangers of failing are at their highest.

While many business owners and managers have suffered in the past few years, at least their experiences are unlikely to be repeated to the same extent by the next wave of small businesses –although there will always be some which fall prey to the dangers of excessive borrowings.

## Taxation policies

A government has available to it a wide range of instruments with which to achieve its economic objectives, including fiscal or taxation policies. Taxation can be split between taxes on income and capital (direct taxation), such as income, corporation and capital gains tax, and taxes on expenditure (indirect taxation), such as VAT. These and other taxation policies can be manipulated, in combination with the use of other measures such as interest rates, in order to stimulate or curtail, for example, consumer spending or levels of investment.

The Budget in 1991 was described by the Chancellor as a 'Budget for business'. Rates of corporation tax were reduced, the profit limit for the 25 per cent small companies rate of corporation tax was increased and companies were allowed to carry back trading losses to offset against taxable profits for three years instead of one. The most unexpected measure, perhaps, was the raising of the standard rate of Value Added Tax from 15 per cent to 17.5 per cent.

The 1992 Budget, on the other hand, was described as a 'Budget for the recovery', and contained few measures which were expected by those outside the government to have any significant effects for either consumers or businesses. The most notable were probably the introduction of a new 20 per cent rate of income tax on the first £2,000 of taxable income, and the effective abolition of inheritance tax on private businesses, farms and unquoted trading company shares.

What were the main effects which might have been anticipated by businesses, and especially smaller ones, as a result of these two Budgets? How would the Budget proposals affect the domestic economy, and should business owners and managers have revised plans or expectations in any particular areas as a result?

Obviously, the Budget proposals need to be considered in conjunction with other economic indicators at that time. So far as the 1991 Budget was concerned, the annual rate of inflation at that time was over 8 per cent, having fallen from its highest level in October 1990 of over 10 per cent. The current account of the balance of trade figures was expected to show a deficit of £6 billion, falling from an estimated deficit for the previous year of some £13 billion. In short, prospects for the UK economy were believed to be improving, and the Chancellor described the Budget as 'good for business, good for families . . . and good for the country'.

The increase in VAT of 2.5 per cent had little impact on business transactions *per se* for VAT registered businesses supplying standard-rated goods. For example, a shop purchases goods at £10 each net of VAT (gross £11.50), and sells them at £20 net of VAT (gross £23.00). No change in net purchase or selling price is made after the VAT increase. The effect on the profit and loss account after the VAT increase is nil, because the figures are stated net of VAT. The effect on cashflow is also nil:

|  | At 15% | At 17.5% |
|---|---|---|
| Cash receipt from sale | 23.00 | 23.50 |
| Less : Cash payment for purchase | 11.50 | 11.75 |
| Net payment of VAT to HMC&E | 1.50 | 1.75 |
| Cash balance remaining | **£10.00** | **£10.00** |

However, the impact on a non-VAT-registered end-user, be this a business or, more likely, an individual consumer, is an increase in price. Should the shop simply assume that the effective price increase should be passed on to the consumer, and that the consumer will continue to purchase at the higher price? Or should the business consider absorbing some or all of the increase itself? Clearly, this will have an adverse effect on the profit and loss account, but is it a necessary measure to maintain levels of demand? This will depend to some extent on the price sensitivity of the goods in question. Price sensitivity refers to the degree to which demand for a product or service decreases in response to an increase in price. Certain goods such as basic foodstuffs may be price insensitive in that an increase in price will have little or no negative effect on its demand. On the other hand, an increase in the price of whisky is more likely to lead to a downturn in demand, because it is not regarded as an essential product.

Part of the rationale behind the increase in VAT was that it would provide the government with revenue with which to subsidize the poll tax. The implication was that the consumer would not suffer overall, because the increase in prices of certain goods would be offset by lower poll tax charges. Whether consumers chose to view the changes in this way is less certain, particularly in view of the recent and continuing high levels of inflation at that time.

The changes in rates of corporation tax were broadly described as 'sensible' moves to help relieve some of the pressures on business. The Chancellor stated that one of his objectives was '. . . to encourage enterprise by creating a broadly based tax system that allows markets to do their job with the minimum of distortion and government interference'. This can be interpreted as meaning that the government intended, by reducing a company's corporation tax bill, to increase the resources available to it for re-investment in the company or to pay out as dividends. While it is some time before companies feel the benefit of a reduction in rates of corporation tax, it should be a factor which features in its plans and projections. In spite of this, as far as many small and unincorporated businesses were concerned, no impact would be felt. However, it was clearly hoped that the effect of the reduction would be an increase in investment, which would have a positive effect for all business in a wider sense.

In contrast, the 1992 Budget contained few proposals which would have a direct or significant effect on businesses. By this time, the annual rate of inflation had fallen to just over 4 per cent, and the government felt that economic recovery was imminent. In addition, a General Election was looming.

The main proposal affecting personal taxation – which was intended to leave consumers with a higher level of disposable income – was the introduction of the 20 per cent tax rate on the first £2,000 of taxable income. However, with the bank base rate still at 13 per cent (although it had dropped to 11 per cent by July that year), it is unlikely that consumers felt any significant benefit. Although the government's main aim was still to reduce and keep under control the rate of inflation, many small businesses nonetheless felt that both market and consumer expectations would remain dampened, and that businesses would continue to suffer as a result.

In view of the economic climate in the early 1990s, there has been little positive action that most small businesses have been able to take in response to the annual Budgets. It was hoped, for example, that the reduction in car tax from 10 per cent to 5 per cent in the 1992 Budget would help the ailing motor industry, but improvements in sales of new cars were not significant, with companies and individuals alike tending to delay purchase or use resources for more pressing commitments.

## Inflation

Inflation in the UK is usually measured in the form of an index, such as the retail price index, which provides a guide to average price movements in the economy. Throughout 1991 and 1992, the government stated one of its prime objectives to be the defeat of rates of inflation which were high relative to European averages: these rates are set out in the table overleaf.

High inflation rates had been aggravated by high levels of consumer demand in the economy in the late 1980s following the easy availability of credit to both consumers and business. Rises in prices tend to lead to higher wage demands from employees, in order to avoid a decline in the real value of their wages. This almost invariably leads to an increase in costs which are passed on by manufacturers in the form of higher prices. If, say, exchange

ANNUAL RATE OF INFLATION BASED ON THE
RETAIL PRICE INDEX

|  | 1989 | 1990 | 1991 | 1992 |
|---|---|---|---|---|
| March | 7.88 | 8.10 | 8.24 | 4.03 |
| June | 8.26 | 9.79 | 5.84 | 3.88 |
| September | 7.56 | 10.89 | 4.10 | 3.57 |
| December | 7.71 | 9.34 | 4.47 | 2.58 |

rates fall at the same time, import prices also rise, adding further pressure to the perceived need for higher wages.

Economic discussion on the causes and effects of and remedies for high rates of inflation becomes increasingly complex, but this is unlikely to provide any immediate and practical solutions for the smaller businesses which have suffered the effects of dampened levels of demand. Grave concerns about unemployment in particular have forced many consumers to reappraise their levels of debt, and to attempt to reduce their borrowings and mortgage commitments if they can.

One of the main problems for smaller businesses, which perhaps applies especially to retailers, is to attempt to maintain a reasonable level of turnover and profitability in the face of these pressures. Various strategies have been tried by those selling more expensive goods such as domestic electrical goods and cars, which include interest-free credit terms or deferred payment schemes. The success of such a policy in stimulating demand has not been proved, and additionally, the retailer is likely to lose out in cash terms: if, for example, the cost of credit is not borne by the consumer, then presumably it has to be suffered by the retailer. Others have had to resort to cutting prices: there can be few high streets which do not bear signs of these sometimes desperate measures in the form of 'Prices slashed' and 'Lowest prices ever' notices in shop windows.

If properly assessed, these strategies may bring a measure of success in helping to prevent the business from going under. However, it should always be remembered that there is no point in reducing prices to such a degree that insufficient cash is generated with which to maintain the business. If, for example, more favourable prices can be negotiated with suppliers, it may be possible to calculate selling price reductions which do not have a damaging effect on either profitability or cashflow. If, however, purchase prices and business overheads remain at a constant level, any reduction in selling prices needs to be calculated extremely carefully.

Smaller retail concerns may be the first businesses to experience these problems, but they are inevitably passed along the chain to wholesalers and manufacturers, although there is usually a time lag before this occurs. Can these businesses therefore use the retail price index as a reliable warning sign of a reduction in demand in the near future? Although indices are potentially useful indicators of average price movements in the economy, they can also be misleading if business owners and managers use them to assess specific decisions within specific markets. The retail price index cannot provide information about changes in the spending habits of any particular household or in any particular sector of the economy. It therefore follows that the use of any general index in decision-making can be of only limited value.

How then can business owners and managers reasonably take account of inflation when trying to assess plans for the future? It has been argued that experience and informed estimates are as useful as strictly adhering to the indicators provided by price indices, although the latter are probably useful as starting points. If, for example, the retail price index has shown an annual rate of inflation for the past six months of 5 per cent, then it is likely that employees will anticipate wage increases slightly in excess of 5 per cent, in order that they feel they are benefiting in real terms, rather than simply keeping pace with inflation. On the other hand, it may be known that a certain supplier of materials will not be instituting the usual increase in prices, in an attempt to stimulate sales. Clearly, it is impossible to build in highly accurate estimates of inflation when trying to project future trading performance, but this should not be used as a reason for projecting, say, a blanket 5 per cent increase in all prices – both of sales and purchases. Educated estimates for specific items together with discreet research will probably be more accurate.

Clearly, inflation represents another area of uncertainty for businesses, and for this reason should not be ignored.

## The effects of recession on expectations

No amount of historical analysis or declared government intention can ever fully account for the expectations and subsequent actions of markets, businesses or individuals. The October 1987 Stock Market Crash was a prime example of this: as *Business* magazine subsequently explained, markets had reached the point 'at which reason and experience in the form of historical evidence and the cycles of economic activity are discounted, and a particularly optimistic psychology captures the market. Once it had taken hold, many of the players came to believe that the market had to continue going up and up.'

The same could be said of the domestic property market at that time. Buyers were committing themselves to borrowings whose monthly repayments represented higher and higher proportions of their income. Again there was a misplaced expectation that prices would continue to rise and that investing in property was safe. As many buyers were later to discover, markets can fall as well as rise, and those who had purchased at or near the peak found themselves either unable to sell their property or to afford the repayments as interest rates rose in late 1988 and 1989.

In a period of prolonged recession, the opposite tends to happen to expectations. Individuals become more cautious in their spending, particularly if they fear for their job security. Expenditure on non-essential goods and services such as holidays, new cars and so on is reduced first. Inevitably, businesses – and usually smaller ones first – begin to feel the effects, and turnover falls. Individuals are less inclined to take risks, such as investing in property, if they feel unsure about their ability to meet mortgage payments. Declarations that economic conditions are improving are often greeted by a sceptical re-action, and even statistics such as falling rates of inflation take some time to provoke higher levels of confidence.

It can be argued that such pessimistic expectations are often self-fulfilling: if, for example, consumers fear unemployment as a result of recession, they are likely to reduce expenditure and increase saving. As a result, retail sales fall, affecting both retailers and those businesses which supply and manufacture goods. Those businesses may need to cut costs as a response to the depressed level of sales, and the measures they adopt may include staff redundancies. Both consumer and business confidence decline further, and so the vicious circle can continue. Clearly, this is something of a simplification of economic behaviour, given the many other factors which play a role in levels of economic activity and growth. However, confidence and expectations in the domestic economy do play a significant role, however rational or otherwise they may be.

Again, it is difficult for businesses affected, either directly or indirectly, by a drop in retail sales, to respond positively in a climate of such uncertainty. Some, such as manufacturers, may be in a stronger position, in that it might be possible to adapt products or processes for other uses. However, the retailers at the end of the chain who are entirely reliant on sales to individuals in the high street may have very limited options, and many have been forced into closure throughout the recession of the early 1990s.

For all businesses finding themselves victims of a drop in sales, it is essential to recognize this as a major problem. Simply hoping that trade will improve is probably the worst course of action. Similarly, small improvements in government statistics after a prolonged period of recession should not be regarded as a sign that poor trading and financial results will be reversed. For example, the retail sales figures in January 1993 showed an increase of 1.6 per cent, compared with an unexpected drop of 1 per cent in December 1992. The January increase was the highest since July 1991 and was described by the Chancellor as 'extremely encouraging'. However, it could be argued that the improvement is not surprising in view of the January Sales: perhaps consumers had simply been delaying their planned purchases in order to take advantage of any further price reductions. Furthermore, the bank base rate cuts in late 1992 and early 1993 meant that many consumers were enjoying the benefit of significant reductions in mortgage repayments, which left them with a higher level of disposable income – or in a stronger position to repay past debts, such as credit card commitments.

The conclusion should not be automatically drawn that a more positive trend in high street spending will continue after a single month's improvement in statistics, even if this does later prove to be the case.

It should therefore be borne in mind that such statistics are not necessarily an indication of an improvement in the economy as a whole, particularly when the movement is so slight. Regardless of anticipated upturns in economic conditions, it is essential to continue to monitor business performance carefully.

As well as monitoring actual results, it is equally important to revise and update business plans and projections. For example, plans which were six months old and which incorporated increases in sales based on a hoped-for economic upturn which does not materialize obviously require rethinking. It may be that the business owner or manager already has a feel for trading results and prospects for the immediate future, and is aware that trading will not match up to earlier expectations. Under such circumstances, it is obviously necessary to reassess projected results for at least the short-term future to ensure, in particular, that the business's cashflow requirements will be met. The most important point is that businesses should remain aware that any improvement in economic activity and conditions can take some time to have any positive effect on trading for smaller businesses.

The problem of cash-starvation was one suffered by a small partnership which designed layouts and supplied fittings for retail shops. Although turnover had been erratic during the business's infancy in the early 1990s, it had succeeded in remaining afloat and making small profits by means of tight financial control. However, to achieve any real progress the business needed to expand. It was unable to secure any bank funding, because although economic conditions were showing some improvement, the banks approached by the partners remained reluctant to lend to what was essentially still a young and relatively unproven business.

This provided a dilemma for the partners. Without

expanding, they felt that there was little prospect of building up the business to a more profitable and stable level. Very discouraged, they seriously considered a decision to cease trading, although they were loath to give up on a venture in which they had invested enormous efforts in such difficult trading conditions.

## Conclusions

The workings of the domestic economy are necessarily extremely complex, and will be affected by many more factors than those mentioned in this section. The ones discussed above, however, represent some of the issues which have affected and concerned smaller businesses in the UK in the early 1990s. While these businesses are unable to insulate themselves completely against the problems of recession, and especially those such as a drop in turnover, it is still essential to be aware of them.

As a source of external instability, economic recession is probably the single most important 'uncontrollable' factor which a business has both to contend with and plan around. While there may, under certain circumstances, be few obvious positive courses of action open to business owners and managers, this should never be regarded as an excuse to pretend that problems do not exist, or that they will simply go away given sufficient time. As with any other area of the business, recognition of problematic issues and an awareness of their potential effect on the business is often both the most difficult and the most important step to be taken.

# 8. **Looking forward**

There is no doubt that the pressures exerted on both individuals and business during a prolonged period of economic recession are a significant contributory factor in the increased proportion of businesses which are unable to survive. However, there will always be a number of businesses which fail, even in the most favourable economic conditions. It has been argued that it is preferable for certain inefficient and poorly-performing businesses to fail, so that the financial damage suffered by both creditors and those within the business is limited as far as possible.

As well as economic considerations, there are factors within a business which will impinge heavily on its chances of survival or failure. Numerous issues and business problems have been discussed in earlier chapters, some which have serious consequences and others whose effects are likely to be easily remedied without any long-term adverse influence on the business.

In general terms, some of the most important areas over which the business owner or manager can exert considerable influence and which will help to maintain the overall 'health' of a company can be summarized as

- planning
- monitoring
- control

These matters should all be regarded as integral to the running of a business, rather than side issues to be tackled when the business owner or manager can spare the time, and each one has been considered in earlier chapters. It should be stressed that more effective planning, monitoring and control will not in themselves rescue a business which has been in decline for some time or which is already on the brink of failure.

For those businesses which have survived the rigours of a long period of economic recession and particularly of high interest rates, the constructive development of a business and its financial stability must be viewed as vital issues. In short, no business can afford to ignore the need to think ahead and to make a careful and regular assessment of all aspects of its performance.

The checklists which follow give some general guidelines to the type of issues which business owners and managers should be considering on a regular basis, if they are to maximize the potential of the business. The checklists are not intended to be exhaustive, but can be used as a starting point to trigger further questions which are specific to the business.

It should be emphasized that answering Yes to these questions does not guarantee business success or survival, just as answering No is not a guarantee of failure. However, this does not mean that No answers should be dismissed as unimportant: these are likely to point to weaknesses in the business, and should provide a constructive basis for reassessment and improvement in the relevant areas.

## Planning Checklist

- Do you have a clear idea of what you want to
  get out of your business?                           Yes / No
  e.g. to make a decent living?
     to sell the business in 10 years?
     to become a market leader?

- Have you a clear idea of how to achieve your
  aims?                                               Yes / No

- Have you prepared a business plan/projections?      Yes / No

- Are your plans/projections regularly updated?       Yes / No

- Are your plans communicated to those who
  play a key role in the business (including
  external advisers)?                                 Yes / No

- Are staff skills maximized and do you delegate
  appropriately and effectively?                      Yes / No

- Are your plans/projections compared with
actual results? Yes / No

- If results do not match up to expectations, are
the reasons identified and remedial action
taken where appropriate? Yes / No

- If results exceed expectations, are the reasons
identified and capitalized upon? Yes / No

- Are plans amended in the light of new
developments? Yes / No

## Monitoring Checklist: Financial

- Is business performance assessed on a regular
basis
e.g. management accounts? Yes / No

- Do you know what gross margins you expect
to achieve? Yes / No

- Are gross profit margins satisfactory? Yes / No
  – compared with prior periods/
  expectations?
  – compared with competitors?
  If not,
  is your product/service suitably priced? Yes / No
  are your direct costs reasonable? Yes / No

- Are your overheads reasonable? Yes / No
  compared with expectations?
  compared with prior periods?

- Are debts collected in accordance with credit
terms? Yes / No

- Is full advantage taken of credit terms from
suppliers? Yes / No

- Is stock turning over sufficiently quickly? Yes / No

- Are assets used effectively? Yes / No

- Are increases in finance requirements discussed
  with bankers *before* they are needed?                    Yes / No

## Monitoring Checklist: Product

- Have you identified a target market and
  understood its needs?                                     Yes / No

- Do you understand your customers' perception
  of your product?                                          Yes / No
  its quality / performance?
  its price?
  its strengths (e.g. reliability, promptness,
  durability)?
  its weaknesses?                                           Yes / No

- Has the level of complaints / problems with
  your product increased/decreased? Are
  complaints / problems followed up and
  resolved?                                                 Yes / No

- Are customer needs reviewed regularly, so that
  repeat business is maximized?                             Yes / No

- Has your customer base increased in the past
  year?                                                     Yes / No

- In the light of the above, do you have plans to
  enhance your product?
  expand / reduce your product range?
  innovate new products?                                    Yes / No

- Where appropriate, have you considered the
  need for patents, trademarks or licences?                 Yes / No

## Control Checklist

- Do adequate accounting and recording systems
  exist?                                                    Yes / No

- Do adequate systems of administration exist?             Yes / No

- Do you pursue an active debt-collection policy?      Yes / No

- Is cashflow actively managed?      Yes / No

- Are successes and problems discussed with key
     personnel and all affected employees?      Yes / No
  e.g. sales?
       marketing?
       finance/performance?

- Are employees working productively and
     efficiently?      Yes / No

- Do you set standards or targets for employees
     and/or production?      Yes / No

- Do you set standards or targets for financial
     performance?      Yes / No

Above all, it should never be forgotten that in the majority of small businesses, it is the business owner or manager who is likely to have the greatest impact on its success or otherwise. It is worth re-iterating that bad management plays an enormously important role in a vast number of business failures.

Even if business decline is a result of economic factors which are beyond the control of the owner or manager, active steps can still be taken to minimize the financial damage. The most important of these are to know how to recognize the problem at an early enough stage, to acknowledge its existence and to identify remedial action quickly – even if this results in the winding up of the business before it declines so far into debt that personal financial ruin is the final outcome. To continue trading in the blind hope that 'things will improve' is a common enough reaction, but may also be the quickest route to personal disaster.

Clearly, winding up a business in which an individual has invested considerable time, energy and money is a distressing process, particularly when job prospects in the immediate future may at best look uncertain. However, it may be considerably less distressing than continuing to incur liabilities which may eventually have to be satisfied personally. Obviously, before initiating such a step, professional advice should be sought, to determine whether this is the most constructive solution under the business's specific circumstances.

Statements are often heard to the effect that the businesses which survive periods of economic recession emerge 'fitter and leaner', more tightly controlled and able to operate more competitively and effectively when economic conditions do improve. This view tends to attract considerable scepticism from those whose businesses have not survived, those who have suffered redundancy as part of the fitness measures and the many whose business performance has declined in spite of vigorous efforts to maintain profitability and stability.

Business owners and managers *can* take active measures to promote the survival chances of their businesses – and those which succeed, particularly under difficult conditions, should not under-estimate their achievement.

## Further reading

Edward I Altman *Corporate Financial Distress – A Complete Guide to Predicting, Avoiding and Dealing with Bankruptcy*. John Wiley & Sons 1983.

John Argenti *Corporate Collapse – the causes and symptoms*. McGraw-Hill Book Company (UK) Limited 1976.

David Clutterbuck and Sue Kernaghan *The Phoenix Factor – Lessons for Success from Management Failure*. Weidenfeld & Nicolson 1990.

John Freear *The Management of Business Finance*. Pitman Publishing 1987.

Colin Gray *The Barclays Guide to Managing Growth in the Small Business*. Basil Blackwell Ltd 1991.

Rebecca Nelson with David Clutterbuck (eds) *Turnaround – How twenty well-known companies came back from the brink*. Mercury Books 1988.

Michel Syrett and Chris Dunn *Starting a Business on a Shoestring*. Penguin Books 1988.

Sara Williams *Lloyds Bank Small Business Guide*. Penguin Books 1992.

Peter Wilson *The Barclays Guide to Financial Management for the Small Business*. Basil Blackwell Ltd 1990.

# Index